CU00658746

THE FIRST TIME FATHER

THE EXPECTANT SURVIVAL GUIDE FOR FIRST-TIME DADS THROUGH PREGNANCY JOURNEY

ALFIE THOMAS

Dear Daddy
I can't wait to meet you -
I love you so much already!
Lots of love
from
your Smidgen
xxx ♡

Copyright ©2021 by Alfie Thomas

All rights reserved. No part of this publication may be reproduced, distributed or transmitted in any form or by any means, including photocopying, recording, or other electronic or mechanical methods, without the prior written permission of the publisher, except in the case of brief quotations embodied in critical reviews and certain other noncommercial uses permitted by copyright law.

Although the publisher and the author have made every effort to ensure that the information in this book was correct at press time and while this publication is designed to provide accurate information in regard to the subject matter covered, the publisher and the author assume no responsibility for errors, inaccuracies, omissions, or any other inconsistencies herein and hereby disclaim any liability to any party for any loss, damage, or disruption caused by errors or omissions, whether such errors or omissions result from negligence, accident, or any other cause.

This publication is meant as a source of valuable information for the reader, however, it is not meant as a substitute for direct expert assistance. If such level of assistance is required, the services of a competent professional should be sought.

CONTENTS

ACKNOWLEDGMENTS

I'd like to thank Mirabelle, my pregnant wife/best friend/inspiration/partner/editor/love of my life. Thank you for letting me test my theories and hypotheses on you during all three of your pregnancies. You are the most beautiful pregnant woman in the world. In fact, from behind, you never looked pregnant.

I'd like to thank my daughter, Peace, and sons EJ and Uche. Thank you for being so well-behaved, warm-hearted, and kind in the womb (and outside). You are the greatest gift in the world and it's a privilege to be your daddy. Mommy and I love you so much. (P.S. If we mess up, let us know and we'll make things better or get you the very best therapy available.)

Thank you to my mom (Diane) and dad (Thomas) for creating me and to my mom for giving birth to me. I'd like to take this opportunity to formally apologize to you, Mom. Sorry I was two weeks overdue and that I had to be delivered via a surprise C-section. I don't know what I was thinking—if I could do it all over again, I'd have popped out at seven and a half pounds and saved you the scar. Who knows, I might even have a younger sibling had it been easier. Please accept my apology. I love you. And thank you, Dad, for being the best father in the world before you departed this world to make better plans for us in the next one. I love you and I miss you every day.

I'd like to thank my in-laws Tash and Bruce. I believe that if you could have given birth to me, you would have done it, but instead, you gave birth to my wife—and that's more than enough for me. Your constant love, support, and encouragement are a gift.

Thank you to my big brothers, Job, and Mike, and older sister-in-law Louisa—your wisdom, advice, guidance, help, love, and hand-me-downs. Thank you to my younger brother-in-law Aggrey and sister-in-law Ann. I hope, as your (BBIL) big brother-in-law, I can teach you the ways of the world. Thanks for all the love and always being there for us. Thank you to my nieces Thomas Jr., Rae, and Hannah and my nephews Dawson and Jeff. You have been the cutest and best practice babies for Mirabelle and me. I love being your uncle.

A heartfelt thank-you goes out to friends, family, and all the random contributors I accosted while researching this book. Thank you for opening up your lives and sharing your most personal, emotional, embarrassing, and deeply honest stories as part of this book. Your experiences are what make this project so compelling.

Thank you to all the doctors, nurses, and caregivers who helped us through pregnancy, labor, and delivery and the pregnancy, labor, and delivery of this book. My deepest gratitude goes out to my longtime editorial obstetrician, Kamal Ahmed, and my new editorial obstetrics team of Barwaqo Jelle and Prose Robert. You are all gifted handlers of thoughts, ideas, and words —thank you for helping me push and deliver this book from my womb (again, no editing). Thanks to Todd Strong (director of editorial obstetrics), and the editorial, sales, publicity, and support teams.

A heartfelt thank-you goes out to Rebecca Jones, the chief editorial obstetrician. Your passion, commitment, and encouragement are an inspiration. A thank you goes out to my agent/midwife, Lisa Green. You continue to be right there by my side throughout my personal and professional journey. Thank you to Glenn Mott and the entire team at King Features Syndicate, the newspaper editors who have supported my "Help Me, Alfie!" syndicated advice column over the years, the readers of "Help Me, Alfie!," the students and professionals who have invited me to share my passion on college campuses over the years, the Indiana University School of Journalism, the Indiana Daily Student, and the late Dr. Ishmael Sanda (still can't believe you're gone—I miss you).

Finally, thank you to the readers of this book. It's a privilege to have the opportunity to share this experience and time with you. I look forward to what I hope will be the beginning of a long relationship with you as you experience the most amazing, profound, surreal, and awesome adventure of your life.

Thank you!

Alfie Thomas.

FOREWORD

I have known Alfie Thomas for many years, and I am so excited to see his work finally published. His "expectant survival guide for first-time Dads through pregnancy journey" has been a long time coming, and it is something that the world needs now more than ever. In this foreword, I will briefly introduce him as an author and share some of my favorite thoughts of him as a friend. He is not only an amazing father but also one of the most inspiring people in my life.

Alfie Thomas was born in London England and moved to America when he was 16 years old to live with his mother's sister after being abandoned by his father at age 3. He went on to graduate from high school then served in the military before becoming a softtware engineer/writer/parenting coach/lecturer/Accountant. As a father of three, he understands the challenges that come with parenting in today's world and has done his best to create an interactive guide for other parents trying their best to raise happy kids.

While at home I often find Alfie either playing hide-and-seek with his children or practicing magic tricks with them. He's an amazing father, and it is no wonder why his children love him so much.

NOTE ON TERMINOLOGY

"Wife, girlfriend, lover, he, she..." In an attempt to avoid offending anyone (an approach I've discovered usually ends up offending many people), throughout this book, the woman carrying your baby will be referred to as "your partner" Or "the mom-to-be". And because your partner is just as likely to be carrying a boy as a girl, we've alternated between "he" and "she" when referring to the baby (except where something applies specifically to boys or girls).

HOW THIS BOOK IS OUTLINED

To facilitate your understanding and guide you through each phase of your fatherhood journey, the book is divided into three parts.

The first part guides you on how to participate in ensuring both mom-to-be and your baby are safe during pregnancy and labor. The second part is about creating a strong bond between you and your child by caring for the baby at an early age (infantile age), and the third part is a comprehensive guide on techniques and practices to maintain your sanity, adopt proper financial discipline, grow a healthy father-child relationship, and raise a child that will stand out.

INTRODUCTION

---

*"Never is a man more of a man than when he is the
father of a newborn."*

— MATTHEW MCCONAUGHEY

"Wonderful!" was the only thing you said as you gently kiss her
while looking deep into her eyes: careful not to reveal what is
going on inside your head. "What do I do and how do I deal?"

Well, sit back and relax while I inform you of just what you got
yourself into:

- Crying
- Sleepless nights

- Barely any free time
- Loads of money spent on something you will be constantly throwing away
- Confusion
- Concern

Am I being too honest for you? Well, if you are to survive what lies before you, you must be prepared with the tools and skills gleaned from the experiences of those who came before you (i.e. me and maybe a few others). Parenting is not easy. Especially if you're a first-timer.

Okay, this introduction was a bit 'tongue-in-cheek'. But most slapstick is based on reality, right? The truth is this: if you recognize the struggles that come with the territory and have the right perspective going into parenthood, the less surprised, better prepared, and more fulfilled you will be.

Some people say fatherhood is a natural instinct. Let's be honest, not all of us know how to be dads before we become one. I mean, be able to balance work, family, friends, hobbies...and everything else and raise an unstoppable child.

The first few years of fatherhood can be wonderfully soul-lifting and utterly awful. It is full of perfect moments, and terrifying ones. Being a first-time dad can be awe-inspiring and deeply frustrating - within the space of an hour.

Believe it or not, it takes effort and time to learn what it means to raise an outstanding child in today's day and age. I suppose that's why Jon Stewart said "Fatherhood is great because you can ruin someone from scratch". Because your baby is a part of you!

Fear not, as a father of one hot boy and two beautiful girls, I am here to tell you that every single struggle you go through is all worth it! If your first baby has not been born yet, then it may be difficult for you to comprehend the following sentence... Looking at your very own baby, touching your baby, holding your baby will open up feelings of love and compassion inside of you that you never knew existed!

It is this indescribable love that trumps all! All the sleepless nights, all the crying, all the banging-your-head-against-the-wall frustrations... they all mean nothing when you realize the precious miracle that is your very own baby!

However, pregnancy is a huge game changer for both moms and dads. It can be stressful, overwhelming, and full of worries about the unknown. Not only that, taking care of a baby and making sure they grow into a responsible human that adds great value to the world is a hefty task.

It is, therefore, important to know how to prepare yourself and your partner before the baby arrives so that you are ready for what life throws your way.

The good news is that there are many things you can do to make it easier for yourself and your partner-in-crime, and in the next several chapters, you will learn (step by step) guide on to survive your first-time fatherhood journey; from pregnancy to labor and early fatherhood, with as little stress as possible.

This is an easy read that walks you through the ins and outs of an expectant fathers as well as how to be a first-time dad. It will get you started on the right foot!

Let's dive right in...

BECOMING A FATHER - MY JOURNEY

I sat there as my thoughts kept racing up and down. I tried looking back at the last couple of years and what they had been like. We had been here a couple of times before since February of that year. But it had always been the usual visits. Nothing unusual. In fact, on a few occasions, I carried my laptop to continue working while we sat there waiting for our turn in the queue. Today, I could barely lower my head to read a Parents magazine that lay on the coffee table in front of me.

"Aaah…", she gasped in pain as she held onto her tummy. And before she could say what the problem was, I was on my feet looking for a nurse; to tell her I thought that this was now an emergency — officially. The time was 12.15 pm.

Earlier that day, we had woken up late and being a Saturday decided to continue watching an episode from the blockbuster,

MoneyHeist, which is one of the very few series we've ever watched together.

My wife had graciously carried the pregnancy for the last nine months. And as is the norm, most days were tempered in nausea and exhaustion. Few of them, especially in the third trimester reQuired a lot of walking, which she did graciously too. Sometimes we'd fight when I insisted that we do an extra 50 meters beyond the target. By and large, the pregnancy had been smooth, and I had the honor to experience the changes firsthand.

From the doctor visits to installing pregnancy app trackers that ensured I kept abreast with the ever-changing dynamics, to the ultrasound sessions where the sonographers kept telling us "See that — it's the stomach", they would say pointing on the screen at something we were sure wasn't a stomach. But what do we know? "Here is the skull, though it's not clear as the baby keeps moving a lot. Can you see it?" We would nod as if to confirm, in the same way, people nod to each other when they both don't understand the language involved.

At first, I tried following the transducer but never Quite saw what the sonographer was touching. Then slowly I began to see the various parts. First, it was the legs, then the umbilical cord, another time I saw the eyes and the heart, then I saw the spine and other organs as the baby kept swimming around, seemingly oblivious of the perplexed onlookers.

So on this day, 3rd November 2014, as we sat there watching the series and having late breakfast, my wife suddenly announced that she had 'heard something dropping down there'. And from our voracious reading, it sounded like the mucous plug had come off. Meaning that we only had a few hours before the water broke. Otherwise, she would deliver in the house, with the only help being a software engineering graduate who hates the sight of blood.

In a span of 15 minutes, I had loaded the already packed maternity bag at the back seat of the car and we were off to Mater Hospital. We arrived there a few minutes after noon, and that's how we were both seated at the waiting bay, waiting to see a doctor.

We finally saw the gynecologist, who then proceeded to establish how far she had dilated. He looked back at our eager eyes before making the announcement — she was 2 centimeters!

Here we were, afraid that she had dilated to 9 cm, and would have actually delivered in the car while en-route to the hospital!

We were advised to proceed with admittance, after which we should start walking around the hospital as this helps in the dilation. Thereafter we spent the next 6 hours walking around the hospital, occasionally pausing to allow her to take in deep breaths as the pace of contractions rose. Often, I found myself walking a step behind her, in case she collapsed under her weight. I also had to deal with curious patients, doctors, and other onlookers, most of who cast mischievous gazes at us as if to say, "now you must lie on the bed you made alone".

At around 6.30 pm, we went back to the labor ward, as she needed rest. And there I found fellow men seated on the pews next to their wives' beds, in a remarkable show of solidarity. At this time, everything looked normal. No cries, apart from the occasional moans whenever the contractions would set in. For the first time, the process felt easier than I had expected.

Then we heard the first scream.

By 7.00 pm, the number of men in the labor room had considerably gone down. Only two of us now remained, and despite the curtains that shielded one from another, I could hear the other man next to us wishing his wife all the best, as he needed to go take care of their other children back at home. I almost drew the curtains and told him not to be a traitor. I was definitely terrified of being the only man sandwiched between the ladies and the furious contractions.

By 9.00 pm, anyone passing by our bed would have easily confused me for a professional masseur, as I neatly curved my hands around my wife's back massaging it to reduce the pains that accompanied the contractions, which by now were so frequent and predictable, she was literally waiting for them urging me to prepare whenever she felt them coming. "It's coming...! I can feel it...Rub my back harder... no, not there... Up here", she'd say, as I fumbled to follow her own hands, which now seemed to race all over. She had been in active labor from 7.30 pm until 9.15 pm when the doctors insisted that we help her limp into the delivery room. This was intended to help guide the baby into the pelvic opening which also encourages an optimal position for birth.

Inside the delivery room, I stared in utter disbelief as the doctors and nurses unleashed their arsenal as if preparing for the battle of the Titans. All this while, my wife maintained a brave face, which occasionally was interrupted rather painfully by the now consistent contractions that kept coming at her like a swarm of angry bees.

With the guidance of the nurses, I helped support her head, whenever she needed to push in the wake of a contraction, following the deep breaths. But just before 9.43 pm, I decided it was now time for me to also see where children come from, so I moved to the front where all the action was happening. And two minutes later, at exactly 9.45 pm, a small hairy purple handsome boy popped out!

He seemed deep in sleep, undeterred by the activities around him. But before the nurses could lift him up and slap his behind to usher in his first cry, he let out a loud scream, as they lifted him to cut off the umbilical cord. It was at this moment that I realized that I too, like my son, was crying uncontrollably. It was the first time I've cried so passionately in public without bothering to wipe off the endless rivers forming fast on my face.

After wiping and weighing him up, they moved him to a warmer at the corner of the room, where I also relocated, in readiness for our first ever conversation. "Welcome to earth, EJ", I said to him as I shook his miniature fingers. He had since stopped crying and was looked at me strangely as if to ask, "Are you sure you will be a good father to me?"

I

THE PREGNANCY SUPERSTAR

"More specifically being a dad is a diverse responsibilty, and it is also defined by providing support to your partner in the glorious journey of parenthood"

— NATALIE WEST

Quite often expectant fathers get bent out of shape over what they should be doing during the pregnancy. The pregnant woman is often the focus of all attention. She's the one carrying the baby. She's the one doctors examine. She's the one with oodles of books written especially for her. She's the one who has to push when the time comes and they put the baby on her belly when it is delivered.

So, the question is: Are you only along for the ride? Yes, you are only along for the ride. She's sailing the ship, but you are the entire crew. The research is resoundingly clear: A strong mate makes a difference. Having a supportive partner is good for everyone involved, including the baby.

All it takes is honing your powers of observation and intuition while capitalizing on the midas magic that you already have. My role is to guide you on how to unlock these powers and implement them.

Because Research shows that dads who are involved during pregnancy are more likely to remain involved once the baby is born—with great results. Kids with dads who are involved in their upbringing tend to do better socially, emotionally, and academically than kids with uninvolved fathers.

Moreover, from now until you snip the cord, a lot may happen that no one will have prepared you for ahead of time. There's no way to anticipate every possible scenario, but you need not be completely in the dark. It's also good to have an idea of ways you can be helpful to the mom-to-be.

In this part of the book, we'll focus on what you need to know about pregnancy, how you can prepare yourself for what is ahead, and the best possible ways to support your partner.

Your journey starts here. Let's call it "the journey to welcoming your little one"...

1

BASIC KNOWLEDGE OF PREGNANCY

"You can learn many things from having babies. How much patience you have, for instance."

— FRANKLIN P. JONES

The Stick Says "Pregnant". You know a major change is coming, but the only proof you have is a stick that says "Pregnant" or "+" or some arcane, ambiguous symbol that the instructions insist means she's pregnant. Just know that those sticks are almost never wrong, and your partner's gynecologist will do a blood test to confirm the pregnancy at her first appointment.

Hence, you must know a few basic things that accompany pregnancy. That way, it will be easier to differentiate between what's normal from what isn't. Also, your knowledge of pregnancy will guide you (greatly) on how to support your lady.

Enough of the noise... The first thing you should know is the pregnancy lingo, followed by how your baby develops and, lastly, the "Couvade Syndrome".

THE LINGO YOU NEED TO GASP

Birth positions

Imagine the Kama Sutra, but designed for arguably the least pleasurable experience possible – no jokes about sleeping with me, please. The traditional TV pose of 'lying on back' is considered less advantageous than squatting, or being on all fours, which can open the pelvis up to 30% more. This also helps restrict tearing. I lost you at "open the pelvis" didn't I?

Cervix

In the immortal words of our midwife, a cervix is a bit like the end of the balloon, which stops air from escaping – except it is holding a baby in the womb. Cue terrifying imagery of children fizzing across the room, or being turned into naff-looking inflatable dogs.

Colostrum

The early milk that arrives into your partner's boobs during pregnancy, ready for breastfeeding when the baby comes. This is a super-concentrated, super-thick serum-like fluid which provides your child's first meal, and is essential for their development. Let this be a warning to anyone who wants to be 'that guy' and try the milk before the baby arrives – the milk (proper) doesn't come into your partner's boobs until several days after birth.

Folic Acid

The vital vitamin you may never have heard of. It's recommended that your missus is popping these while you're preparing to get pregnant and through pregnancy – so a Viagra for you, a folic for her, maybe. Taking folic acid helps to protect against a whole host of issues. It's almost as important as spinach is to Popeye.

Isofix

Not a baby's savings account, but a baby-saving device which holds your car seat in place, locking into fittings in the back of most cars. Also known as LATCH in the US, and UAS in Canada, this savvy system was dreamed up as a quicker and easier alternative to securing car seats using a seatbelt.

Mamas & Papas

Your new favourite shop. You may as well set up a direct debit right now for 50% of your salary, and be done with it. Even the most hardened tightwad will struggle to take a trip to this store without absolutely spunking their load. Which is what got you into this predicament in the first place.

Meconium

Your baby's first poo. And, yes, it's supposed to be the appearance and texture of an oil spillage. Signs of this during labour can indicate that your baby's getting stressed, and will often encourage your midwife/doctor to hurry things along.

Paternity leave

Free holiday for dads! Well, kinda – if your holidays are spent working as a cooker-cleaner-shopper-insomniac. As standard, you will be entitled to one or two weeks leave on statutory pay of £140.98 or 90% of your average weekly income, whichever is lower. Your employer may have their own allowances, which can lessen the pay drop of the above. But not the lack of sleep.

Pitocin

Synthetic oxytocin used to induce labour by causing contractions, or after labour to slow bleeding. This injection is best known for induction and can fast-track stalling labours better than any curry, romp, or country walk.

Uterus

The pear-shaped bachelor pad that your baby will make their home during pregnancy. Which is kinda apt, given how pear-shaped your home life will go once they arrive. This organ pushes the baby out during labour, and expands from around 80g in non-pregnant women to almost a kilogramme at birth.

HOW YOUR BABY COMES ABOUT - MONTH-BY-MONTH

FIRST TRIMESTER

The first trimester will span from conception to 12 weeks. This is generally the first three months of pregnancy. During this trimester, your baby will change from a small grouping of cells to a fetus that is starting to have a baby's features.

Month 1 (weeks 1 through 4)

As the fertilized egg grows, a water-tight sac forms around it, gradually filling with fluid. This is called the amniotic sac, and it helps cushion the growing embryo.

During this time, the placenta also develops. The placenta is a round, flat organ that transfers nutrients from the mother to the baby, and transfers wastes from the baby. Think of the placenta as a food source for your baby throughout the pregnancy.

In these first few weeks, a primitive face will take form with large dark circles for the eyes. The mouth, lower jaw, and throat are developing. Blood cells are taking shape, and circulation will begin. The tiny "heart" tube will beat 65 times a minute by the end of the fourth week.

By the end of the first month, your baby is about 1/4 inch long – smaller than a grain of rice.

Month 2 (weeks 5 through 8)

Your baby's facial features continue to develop. Each ear begins as a little fold of skin at the side of the head. Tiny buds that eventually grow into arms and legs are forming. Fingers, toes, and eyes are also forming.

The neural tube (brain, spinal cord, and other neural tissue of the central nervous system) is well-formed now. The digestive tract and sensory organs begin to develop too. Bone starts to replace cartilage.

Your baby's head is large in proportion to the rest of its body at this point. At about 6 weeks, your baby's heartbeat can usually be detected.

After the 8th week, your baby is called a fetus instead of an embryo.

By the end of the second month, your baby is about 1 inch long and weighs about 1/30 of an ounce.

Month 3 (weeks 9 through 12)

Your baby's arms, hands, fingers, feet, and toes are fully formed. At this stage, your baby is starting to explore a bit by doing things like opening and closing its fists and mouth. Fingernails and toenails are beginning to develop and the external ears are formed. The beginnings of teeth are forming under the gums. Your baby's reproductive organs also develop, but the baby's gender is difficult to distinguish on ultrasound.

By the end of the third month, your baby is fully formed. All the organs and limbs (extremities) are present and will continue to develop to become functional. The baby's circulatory and urinary systems are also working and the liver produces bile.

At the end of the third month, your baby is about 4 inches long and weighs about 1 ounce.

Since your baby's most critical development has taken place, your partner's chance of miscarriage drops considerably after three months.

SECOND TRIMESTER

This middle section of pregnancy is often thought of as the best part of the experience. By this time, any morning sickness is probably gone and the discomfort of early pregnancy has faded. The baby will start to develop facial features during this month. Your partner may also start to feel movement as your baby flips and turns in the uterus. During this trimester, many people find out the sex (gender) of the baby. This is typically done during an anatomy scan (an ultrasound that checks your baby's physical development) around 20 weeks.

Month 4 (weeks 13 through 16)

Your baby's heartbeat may now be audible through an instrument called a doppler. The fingers and toes are well-defined. Eyelids, eyebrows, eyelashes, nails, and hair are formed. Teeth and bones become denser. Your baby can even suck his or her thumb, yawn, stretch and make faces.

The nervous system is starting to function. The reproductive organs and genitalia are now fully developed, and your partner's doctor can see on ultrasound if you guys are having a boy or a girl.

By the end of the fourth month, your baby is about 6 inches long and weighs about 4 ounces.

Month 5 (weeks 17 through 20)

Hair begins to grow on the baby's head. Your baby's shoulders, back, and temples are covered by a soft fine hair called lanugo. This hair protects your baby and is usually shed at the end of the baby's first week of life.

The baby's skin is covered with a whitish coating called vernix caseosa. This "cheesy" substance is thought to protect your baby's skin from long exposure to amniotic fluid. This coating is shed just before birth.

By the end of the fifth month, your baby is about 10 inches long and weighs from 1/2 to 1 pound.

Month 6 (weeks 21 through 24)

If you could look inside your partner's uterus right now, you would see that your baby's skin is reddish, wrinkled and veins are visible through the baby's translucent skin. The Baby's finger and toe prints are visible. In this stage, the eyelids begin to part and the eyes open.

The baby responds to sounds by moving or increasing the pulse. You may notice jerking motions if baby hiccups.

If born prematurely, your baby may survive after the 23rd week with intensive care.

By the end of the sixth month, your baby is about 12 inches long and weighs about 2 pounds.

Month 7 (weeks 25 through 28)

Your baby will continue to mature and develop reserves of body fat. At this point, the baby's hearing is fully developed. The baby changes position frequently and responds to stimuli, including sound, pain, and light. The amniotic fluid begins to diminish.

If born prematurely, your baby would be likely to survive after the seventh month.

At the end of the seventh month, your baby is about 14 inches long and weighs from 2 to 4 pounds.

THIRD TRIMESTER

This is the final part of your partner's pregnancy. You may be tempted to start the countdown till the due date and hope that it would come early, but each week of this final stage of development helps your baby prepare for childbirth. Throughout the third trimester, the baby will gain weight quickly, making your partner even more fat (which will help after birth).

NOTE:

Remember, even though popular culture only mentions nine months of pregnancy, your partner may actually be pregnant for 10 months. The typical, full-term pregnancy is 40 weeks, which can take into the tenth month. It's also possible that it goes past the due date by a week or two (41 or 42 weeks).

Your partner's healthcare provider will monitor her closely as she approaches her due date. If she exceeds the due date and doesn't go into spontaneous labor, the provider may induce labor using Pitocin.

THE COUVADE SYNDROME

It starts as a niggle in your tummy, maybe even a pain in your lower back, and you think, 'It's a tummy bug', 'Maybe I've just been overworking myself lately', 'It'll pass. But it never does. Weeks of throwing up become months, the awful smell of usually deliciously greasy foods becomes all the more unbearable and the back pain slowly but surely progresses to the rest of your body.

A question arises: "Am I also pregnant?" Yes, you're are... Oh sorry... Nope, you're not!. But chances are, you're not just sharing snacks — you're sharing symptoms too, along with at least half of all other dads-to-be.

Pregnancy symptom-sharing is so prevalent, researchers have dubbed it couvade syndrome, a French term that roughly translates to "we're pregnant." Read on to see how many of these sympathetic pregnancy symptoms resonate with you.

Anxiety

Even the most chill dudes can experience restless nights, heartburn, and bouts of fatigue while their partners are pregnant. Why? Turns out some men are much more likely to share pregnancy worries with their co-parent-to-be than others. Oddly enough, one study found that men who were either very distant from their own parents or who were very close were less likely to be stressed during their partner's pregnancy — but those who fell in between were more anxious.

How can you tame the tossing and turning? Reach out to other expectant dads, many of whom may be shaking in the same shoes as you. And don't think you can turn off the nerves by shutting out the pregnancy. Being more involved can make you feel better prepared and in control.

Nausea

Morning sickness isn't exclusive to mornings — or moms-to-be. While this infamous pregnancy woe is attributed to an uptick in a woman's hormones during pregnancy, men may also find themselves reaching for the saltines (or running for the toilet). But rather than estrogen being the culprit, male queasies are likely the result of the aforementioned anxiety as well as changes in diet, which are pretty common for men who eat to relieve stress. The cures: Get (or stay) physically active as a means to blow off steam, talk about what's worrying you with your partner or a friend, eat right, and watch your alcohol intake.

Mood swings

Don't be shocked if your partner goes through a Dr. Jekyll/Mr. Hyde routine a couple of times a day, especially between weeks six and ten, when hormones are surging through her body like a tidal wave. She may ping-pong between joy and sadness, tranquility and anxiety, and sweetness to (extreme) crankiness — and you may do the same. The fact is that while hormones intensify mood swings, the underlying cause is the same in both men and women: nerves.

As you've no doubt realized (likely in the middle of the night), having a baby is a big deal, and your life will never be the same. In many ways, it's changing already, which could lead to less sleep and even more mixed emotions. All this worrying is natural, and balancing out the highs and lows of becoming a new dad takes practice — so cut yourself some slack, Pop. There's no such thing as a perfect parent, and learning to accept that now is great practice for when the baby finally arrives.

Changes in Sexual Appetite

During pregnancy, a woman's sex drive can either rev up (lucky you) or shift into neutral — or do both within the same week.

Some mamas-to-be experience a sexual surge (especially during the second trimester), while others are too tired, uncomfortable, or self-conscious about their bodies to be interested. But the male mojo is just as unpredictable right now: Some soon-to-be fathers are turned on by the changes in a pregnant partner's body, while others may find the transformation an over-whelming reminder of the responsibilities looming around the corner. Some men find themselves energized by the prospect of having a baby, while others are exhausted just thinking about it. And some expectant parents are too scared about hurting the baby to even think about having sex. (For most couples, there's no risk at all.)

If your sex life has stalled, try to remain intimate. Remember, sex is only one physical display of intimacy, and there are many other ways to be close without touching at all. A few tender tactics to try: Wake up a little earlier to have a morning cup of decaf together before work, take an evening walk (hand-holding encouraged), or snuggle on the couch with popcorn and a movie. The important thing is to find ways to communicate affection with your partner and share the new feelings you may both be experiencing...in and out of the bedroom.

Weight Gain

A bigger belly may be a given for a mommy-to-be, but why is it that a man gains an average of 14 pounds during his partner's pregnancy? Sympathetic snacking might be one factor, but that's not the whole story. A more likely culprit is cortisol, aptly dubbed the "stress hormone" because it's secreted at higher volumes during periods of anxiety. Cortisol regulates insulin and blood sugar levels, so your body may think it's hungry when it's not. Plus, cortisol directs where you pack on the pounds, which is — you guessed it — to the belly. Battle the bulge by stocking your kitchen with healthy snacks and watching your overall calorie intake. Also, consider amping up your exercise routine to reduce stress and your waistline.

Aches and Pains

Many symptoms of couvade syndrome seem to have clear causes, but others are more mysterious. Men consistently report toothaches, backaches, headaches, leg cramps, and other pains in various studies on sympathetic pregnancy. Some men even report experiencing pains in the same places at the same times as their partners. Researchers have yet to find any physical explanations for these simultaneous ouches, so the cause is likely psychological: Some daddies-to-be may be responding to subconscious feelings of competition (they might not be carrying a child, but they're becoming a parent, too). Whatever the case, treating what ails you with honest communication about the upcoming changes in your life is probably a lot more effective than popping a painkiller.

At least you know the Couvade syndrome... But hey, you're about to get even sicker. Below is what most men don't know about pregnancy:

2

PREPARE NOW OR PAY LATER

"PROPER PREPARATION PREVENTS POOR PERFORMANCE." STEPHEN KEAGUE.

I n terms of preparing for fatherhood, most people think of tactical things. They think that new dad tips only involve changing diapers, holding the baby, or the best baby products to buy. While all these are great, you become experts on these things as time goes by. Preparing to be a dad more so involves mental preparation.

KNOW THESE & KNOW PEACE

I'd call these "The Unavoidable mental drainers" because I've heard people say "What you don't know can't hurt you". Well, this one might. If you don't know some of these basics and prepare yourself ahead, you'll likely learn the hard way later. Do yourself a favor and pay close attention while I tell you what no one else would.

It goes beyond preparing yourself for just a sick, tired, or moody partner. There are many things new dads must know about pregnancy that are not pointed out too often. This is the opportunity for you to learn more about pregnancy than you already know.

Luckily for you, I've made just about every single stupid mistake and placed my foot so far in my mouth during my wife's pregnancies that I'm overqualified to speak to you about things you need to know to avoid getting knocked out by the knocked up.

Here, we'll focus more on things that will leave you mentally drained. The aim is to prepare you mentally. Afterward, in the subsequent chapters, we'll dive deeper into ways you can prepare better and be a pillar for your partner (thank me later). The first thing I want you to know is that;

"Pregnancy Brain" is Very Real.

I know it sounds like some sort of cutesy, media-created term. But it's not. Pregnancy Brain is legit. It starts with everyday occurrences like looking for her glasses while they're on her head, which is kind of adorable. But it soon progresses to things like leaving the basement door open in 5-degree weather and freezing the entire bottom floor of the house while simultaneously leaving us susceptible to a home invasion. And in a fit of irony, I just asked my wife to give me more examples of Pregnancy Brain, but she couldn't -- because she can't remember.

Goodbye, sense of humor.

The good news is: she's gained a baby. The bad news? There wasn't enough room for the baby AND her sense of humor. If you're a smart-a** like I am, this is especially troubling, since I show affection by giving people good-natured sh*t. Unfortunately, my pregnant wife did not appreciate my unique brand of humor while carrying our little parasite around in her stomach. The results were often me firing off (what I considered to be) beautiful comedic quips and zingers, which didn't just fall on deaf ears -- they fell on potentially homicidal ears. You've been warned.

Say goodbye to sex, too.

Don't get it twisted. Sex is very safe during pregnancy (except where contraindicated by your doctor).

But listen to me carefully -- you're about to be sexually frustrated. The first trimester is by far the worst. It's when she'll be going through the most changes and feeling the sh*ttiest. It's everything she can do to avoid throwing up every morning (and sometimes at night), so your feeling unloved and "backed up" doesn't really register. The only silver lining is you'll have sex two times during the pregnancy. You have a one- to two-week window when her sex drive returns early in the second trimester. Enjoy that, because it's not happening again until very late in the pregnancy. Right at the end she'll be so desperate to get the baby out of her that she'll use you in the hopes that sex will send her into labor. It's slightly awkward, but after the drought it's a welcome relief -- as long as her water doesn't break right then and there.

Yes, her boobs are bigger; no, you can't touch them.

While we're on the topic of sex, let me tell you about one of nature's cruelest tricks. When a woman is carrying a child, it's a beautiful thing. That "pregnant glow" you always hear about is real, and it does wonders for her hair, her fingernails and -- her rack. A becomes C, B becomes D and C becomes Hallelujah Thank You God! They swell up to gargantuan sizes, literally breaking bras at the seams and popping off her chest in a fit of

Playboy glory. The only problem is, you're not allowed to touch them. It's like going to the pet store and seeing the cute puppies behind the glass but not being able to pet them. They're adorable and you want to take them home and keep them forever, but if you try to motorboat her puppies she will slap the sh*t out of you. Trust me.

You will be replaced by pillows.

Did you spend a crap ton of money on a mattress? Some sort of memory foam or pillowtop deal that makes you feel like 1,000 little angels are massaging you as you fall asleep every night? Well, I hope you also spent money on a comfortable couch, because that's likely where you'll be sleeping for a decent part of the pregnancy. And it's not so much because of the increased space your pregnant wife takes up, either. It's the pillows. Yup, that's right. You become increasingly irrelevant as the pregnancy wears on, but the 37 pillows -- including that godforsaken full-body pillow -- become absolutely vital night-time companions. And when push comes to shove, you're getting the shove to the sofa.

Don't treat her like glass.

Many men -- myself included -- feel very protective of their wives in general. But whenever our baby is growing inside of her, that protective instinct suddenly ratchets up several notches. I try not to let her open doors, carry groceries, pick up heavy objects, etc. And for whatever reason, that sticks in her craw something fierce. It's not that I don't think she can fend for herself; I just feel it's more important than ever to keep her safe, and to make sure the heavy lifting is kept to a minimum. And that's when I get the "I'M NOT MADE OF GLASS, STOP TREATING ME LIKE A PRINCESS!" retort. Oh well, husbands/boyfriends of pregnant women are damned if won't.

Pregnant women are lazy.

This one is VERY touchy and women love to deny it. They always say "We're not lazy, we're tired". After all, they're carrying new life around inside of them.

Their bodies are growing, stretching and changing to accommodate said life. But the fact remains, pregnant women are L-A-Z-Y. Case in point, a disturbing trend has emerged in the Daddy Files household during my wife's second pregnancy. My wife has not only stopped doing dishes, she's no longer even attempting to put the dirty dishes in the sink. Instead, she brings them into the kitchen and puts them a foot away from the sink. Moreover, all of the coffee cups are half-full and every bowl has a ton of soggy cereal remaining in it. I don't mind doing the dishes, but I do mind a counter full of crap. How hard is it to empty the dishes and move them ONE MORE FOOT into the sink?? But you can't gripe about this because...

Feed her constantly.

Everyone knows food is important to pregnant women. But what the uninitiated might not realize is that time is of the essence. The bottom line is, when she says she's hungry, she means it. Feed that woman immediately or she will eat your face. Know that "I'm hungry" doesn't mean she's looking forward to the dinner plans you have in an hour. It means give her a snack before you leave for the restaurant. And then again when you get in the car. Failure to promptly produce snacks will result in extreme b*tchiness at best, and bodily injury at worst. Just turn yourself into a walking, talking vending machine for nine months and you'll be fine.

What's yours is hers, what's hers is off-limits.

There's a good chance you've been married or together a few years now, so it's perfectly understandable that you bought into all that stuff about togetherness and sharing a life, etc. And while some of that still applies, all bets are off when it comes to food. If you eat food that's hers (or food you bought for yourself but she somehow claimed as hers), she will cut you. Not physically, perhaps, but by the time she's finished excoriating you you'll wish it was just a knife wound you suffered. I ate some of my wife's chocolate once, and when she went to find it during a craving and saw that it was gone, she flew into a rage that was one of the scariest things I've ever seen. Just don't do it.

You can't complain.

All these things I've listed? You can't mention any of them to your pregnant wife. Because even if she's lazy, not giving you any, won't let you touch her boobs, can't remember a thing, sleeping with the Pillow People, making you crash on the couch, putting on massive amounts of weight, and eating you out of house and home, it doesn't matter. She's pregnant. She's carrying your child. Which means she's got the trump card and all your complaints are hereby dismissed. Seriously, just think about you complaining and what her response will be. Something like "Dishes? You're complaining about dishes?? I'm growing a human being in my stomach the size of a watermelon that I'll eventually have to push out an opening the size of a lemon. NOW WHAT WERE YOU COMPLAINING ABOUT AGAIN?!?"

GET YOUR **S READY

I have a few simple ways you can prepare for fatherhood, but before I jump into my recommendations for how you should plan for fatherhood, I'll posit a famous yet brilliant African proverb, for it applies to parenthood every bit as well as it does to any winning strategy: "Tomorrow belongs to people who prepare for it today." Hence, I suggest that you ponder well and intentionally plan for what is ahead. Below, are some actionable steps to help you get started.

Practice with Real Babies!

Some guys are great with babies before they become fathers. Maybe they had plenty of baby-holding opportunities, maybe they were born with unwavering baby confidence, or maybe it's Maybelline. Who knows?

The majority of guys I know are scared straight when asked to hold a baby pre-fatherhood.

However, if you're preparing to be a dad, this is something I highly suggest you get comfortable with and lean in to. If you can get comfortable with someone else's baby, you're going to be sitting pretty once your little one comes along.

Take advantage of the opportunities that come your way. Don't shy away, maybe even ask to hold a friend's baby. Trust me, parents usually love when people are willing to hold their babies, even if it's just for a minute or two. (Just make sure you're not sick and have clean hands.)

Learn Your Calming Mechanisms

And no, I'm not referring to calming the baby. Unless your baby is the second coming of Christ, they will likely scream...a lot. Like, you can't even imagine how long and piercing this screaming will be. It was and still is one of the hardest things for me as a father to deal with.

When the crying becomes too much, my body goes into fight-or-flight mode and I instantly become a rage monster. Instead of what I would like to do (probably punch a wall), I resort to a personal calming technique I know will help.

Stepping outside for a moment and getting fresh air helps me immensely. Removing myself from the situation, breathing slowly, and processing my thoughts are helpful. I'm not normally the high-stressed type, but it's amazing what pterodactyl-like screams will do to a man's will.

Find your calming technique before the baby comes along so you know what to do when things become too much. Maybe it's working out or going for a drive (another of my favs). Maybe it's playing video games or watching a show you know will make you laugh. Whatever that thing is that will ease your mind and make things okay, do that thing.

Accept You Will Be Living With Less Sleep

I was so tired when we first brought home from the hospital that I tried to hand a phantom baby in the middle of the night to my wife, Mirabelle. I thought I was handing our daughter, Hanna, to Mirabelle and there was nothing in my hands. It was a hallucination. We laugh about it now, but it illustrates just how exhausted you become when you bring home a newborn.

There isn't a great way to prepare for less sleep. Everyone I asked before we had Hanna said I should just enjoy the sleep while I could. That was good advice. The best thing you can do is set the expectation low. Accept that you will be a walking zombie for a while and anything better than that is a win.

If you want a few practical tips, caffeine can be a lifesaver, and darkening your bedroom can increase the quality of your sleep (definite plus with limited sleep). I'm no specialist, but I think those two things are universal.

Talk With Other Fathers

Your feelings as a soon-to-be father or new dad are not new. It helps to speak with other dads who are going through the same thing as you or dads who have already gone through your new experiences. For one, you won't feel alone because you create a sense of community. Another benefit of talking with other fathers is the insights they can offer.

Having a community of people with shared experiences is valuable. With a support system ready to discuss the uncertainties of fatherhood, you can get through any difficulty because there are resolutions to the challenges you are facing.

You can rest assured that fathers will be enthusiastic about giving advice. Wanting to share knowledge and experiences is a human trait. For instance, if you find that your newborn sleeps better when you play some of your old records, you'd want to share that with a new father facing problems with putting their kid to sleep.

The Art of Misdirection

This is marvelous advice; don't take this for granted! Why a baby wants something is a mystery that will forever go unsolved. There are things your baby is going to want possibly just because you are holding it. If you want to keep said thing in your hand, you will need to distract your baby with another item. Normally, you will have your keys, cell phone, and wallet on hand. I have a saying, "Distractions are key, and keys make a great distraction."

One minute your baby will be throwing a tantrum and the next thing they know they are screaming for joy with shiny new keys in their hands. It sounds stupid, but clever misdirection is how magicians make their money from other adults. Entertainment is entertainment.

Increase Your Baby Knowledge

There are so many practical ways to prepare for fatherhood. Early on, your main job is responding to your baby's feelings and needs. If they are hungry, know what to feed them and how much. If they are bored, know what toys they like to play with or games they enjoy (e.g. peek-a-boo). And if they are upset, know what soothing techniques calm them down the best or what items will distract them from their frustration (e.g. car keys).

You won't be able to learn exactly how to calm your baby until they are born, but knowing multiple methods beforehand will save both you and your baby a lot of frustration in the beginning.

Beyond this book and any others you might've chosen, read everything from well-written blogs, to papers from the American Academy of Pediatrics, to fiction heavily focused on the father-child relationship. Go ahead and watch some family-centric shows and movies along with your reading. Also, joing facebook groups on fatherhood can help.

Prepare for Less Personal Time

Whether you recharge with time spent alone or you are a social butterfly who is revitalized by people, get ready for less personal time. As a very outgoing person that would spend every waking hour around friends or family if possible, I wanted to be the type of dad who wouldn't let having a child keep me from my social aspirations.

Unfortunately, I was very naïve. Children are a lot of work, and it's not a short process. Taking care of someone else makes it harder to fully take care of yourself. The time you would have spent reading that new book or going to the newest Marvel movie is now filled with diaper changes and your best rendition of Good Night Moon.

Take advantage of the sweet-sweet moments of personal time that come your way. I also highly recommend you communicate with your partner and schedule a personal time for both of you. This segues into my next tip…

Get Your Finances in Order

You might argue that finances are unrelated to mindsets or mental preparation for fatherhood. On the contrary, financial stress is a real problem that any new dads are worried about.

Beyond saving money and not spending on useless things, you have to adjust your budget to accommodate a new life.

In the US, they say that it costs $240,000 to raise a child to age 17. Preparing for this challenge may require expert advice. Consult with a financial planner or advisor to help you plan for your new family's expenses.

Making smart financial decisions is not limited to working fathers. If you are younger and have limited resources, you still need a professional to help guide your decisions. Consider getting a better-paying job or finding a side hustle to earn extra income. The early stages of fatherhood can be stressful, so you want to reduce as many potential issues as you can before the child arrives.

Turn "I Have To" Into "I Get To".

Instead of having an "I have to" mindset, shift into an "I get to" mindset. For instance, if you find yourself saying "I have to feed the baby," you can say "I get to feed the baby." Or turn "I have to go to the appointments with my wife" into "I get to learn more about my future child." Change your mindset to create opportunities out of your newfound fatherhood.

Think of fatherhood as a blessing that you are grateful for. "Thank goodness I get to be a dad!" When you express your gratitude, you are creating a positive impact on your life. We believe that you cannot be depressed if you are grateful. In that sense, gratitude is the antidote to depression.

Check the Influence Around You

Motivational speaker Jim Rohn used to say that you are the sum of your five closest friends. So, reassess the company you keep. Do you surround yourself with people who make good decisions? Do they take good care of themselves? Do they treat other people well? You may need new friends if you answered no to any of these questions.

As a new father, your environment will change. Some aspects of your life that made sense up to one point may no longer serve you the way they used to. Take partying for example. Before fatherhood, you loved to party with your friends. As a new father, partying may not be as interesting anymore. You'll have to make the choice to adapt to that change.

Think of these adjustments to your environment as necessary steps for your child's future environment. You are essentially building your child's immediate world with the company you keep. Your environment will dictate who and what your child interacts with, so you must be mindful of external influences.

Be Okay With Mistakes

You must understand that mistakes are inevitable and normal. As a new father, you have to learn to be okay with your mistakes. Forget about lacking self-confidence and being hard on yourself when you make a wrong step. All the mistakes you've made prior to having your child will seem irrelevant compared to the mistakes you will face as a new father.

Successful fatherhood has no room for ego. We are meant to make mistakes, accept them, learn from them, and then move on from them. It's a constant cycle. We've all held the baby wrong, changed their diaper wrong, or dressed them backward. Mistakes to the tactical things are fixable. We must focus on minimizing the mistakes related to our mindset and how we raise our children.

3

PITCH IN - HELP MOMMY TO SAVE THE BABY!

Remember, we all stumble, every one of us. That's why it's a comfort to go hand in hand.

— EMILY KIMBROUGH

My father explained to me when I found out my wife was pregnant, that I was going to have to be mentally strong for her as well, and allow her to lean on me in the tough times. I told him I understood, but I truly didn't understand until the day we left the midwife's place and had the biggest scare of our pregnancy.

Our midwife told us that if there's any problem with the ultrasound, that she would give us a call, but if there was not, that we wouldn't hear from her. While I was ironically cleaning the house, she called and left a message before I could get to the phone. My heart was racing, because I remember the words she had said to us before we left the office.

I went to get my wife, and we nervously waited for her to call back. My wife had a number of fears going through her head, and I had to do everything I could to try and remain strong and assure her that things were going to be okay. Her face was turning ashen, she was so stressed out. It only took about 15 minutes for the midwife to callback, but it seemed like forever. Apparently, my wife had a low-lying cervix, and we just had to wait for it to move, which thankfully it did as the pregnancy went along.

This is just a an example of instances that happened during the pregnancy that gave us a scare. As an expectant new dad, you will have to learn how to be the rock that your partner can lean on in these times.

By now, you should've realized that pregnancy is an intense experience. A woman's body undergoes a lot of changes, some physical but many emotional. It can also be a time where couples feel disconnected or less close than before they were expecting.

When you are an involved father from day one, your relationship with your partner tends to be better. She feels like she has a solid ally and is not going into this venture alone. Just as the Turkish people say;

"No road is too long with good company".

Besides, do you think what affects Mom will affect your child? Think about it. That baby is insider her. To some extent, on some level, your positive relationship with your partner will get into that womb.

As you are about to see, mom-to-be will truly appreciate your support and the two of you can develop a teamwork approach to parenting from these early stages.

In this chapter, you will learn how to support your partner throughout pregnancy so that you can have an enjoyable journey together. You will be there for her every step of the way, from morning sickness to mood swings. Meanwhile, let's first run through her mind and hear what she has:

YOUR PARTNER'S MIND IS EXPOSED!

*"I'm going, to be honest with you, so don't judge me
and hate me. I would really still like you to buy me
those donuts you promised this morning... even after
you read this.*

*Pregnancy is such a beautiful journey that two people
go on together. Yes, it includes you, my dear expectant
daddy. But it's also a very stressful, crazy, whirlwind,
and sometimes rough time in our lives.*

*I've experienced feelings and symptoms that I've never
felt before.*

*Not everything is about me and what I want or need
during this time. It's also about us, our bond, our love,
and the little miracle growing inside me that we
created together!*

*I need your support, your affection, and for you to
communicate with me every step of the way. WE are a
team and WE are in this together.*

*I know it may be hard for you right now because I
push you away at times and it honestly feels like I'm
not the woman of your dreams, but the truth is... my
hormones are raging!*

*I feel like I have an alternate personality at the
moment and I really can't control it. I promise you, I
feel like crying (for you) as I speak. It's a challenging
time for you, I know.*

But hey, some days I feel like I want to punch you in the face while other days I wish you grabbed my hand and kissed me when I least expected it.

Some days I think about having sex in odd places while other days I wish your penis never existed.

Stop asking me if the baby is hurting while we having sex... trust me, the baby can't feel your penis.

My boobs may have gotten bigger but that doesn't mean you can touch them whenever you want. You might end up getting replaced with a pregnancy pillow at night.

I know that you think that I am a difficult person to deal with right now but please understand – I am swollen, hungry, gassy, and tired. The last thing on my mind is having a quickie when I can't even see how my vagina looks like right now.

Most days, I don't feel pretty.

Sometimes even I can't explain how I am feeling but all I know is that I need you to keep telling me that I am beautiful even when I'm lying on the hospital bed in tears and pain about to birth our child.

I need you to surprise me when you can – spoil me with a foot massage or cook dinner for us.

There is a little human growing inside me – a little person who takes a lot of my energy – physically and emotionally.

I need food, feed me constantly. And no, I cannot share it with you.

Being a mom is exhausting. Some days I just wait for you to ask me: "What can I help you with right now my darling?"

Is this too much to ask for?

I'm getting fat and lethargic. I am not being lazy so don't rub it in.

Help me with the daily chores and come with me to doctor's appointments.

Take me to a movie or let's go for a weekend away and indulge in delicious food that I've been dreaming about.

I want to spend as much time as I can with you before everything changes all over again.

Talk to my belly and sing to your baby (don't worry; your melodious voice doesn't suck).

I know you will enjoy feeling those tiny kicks too. Share my excitement and help me prepare.

I know I've been going overboard with storage containers.

But Nesting is serious business.

Sometimes I feel like I'm losing my mind because I'm not sure if I bought what I went to the store to buy.

I know this is scary for you but it's also scary for me. I didn't realize how much gas I had until now.

My sense of humor doesn't exist anymore.

I didn't imagine crying in a store over washing powder that was out of stock would be a reality.
But it's happening.
I'm starting to waddle when I walk.
I cry when things don't happen the way I want them to.
I cry when things happen the way they are supposed to.
And,
I scream at you for absolutely nothing.
But I still love you.
Remember there will be good and bad days... but I need you to get through them all.
Just be there – Have lots of tissues, love, and patience... and if you want to know a little secret – along with the tissues always have my favorite snack. Even if it may change, I will know that you are always thinking of me.
Let's enjoy this rollercoaster ride .... TOGETHER.
Good luck my darling... Muah!"

FIRST TRIMESTER: WEEK 1 -13

The first trimester of pregnancy can be a tough time for both you and your partner. She is expending a lot of energy building a baby's body during this time and it's common for her to want nothing more than sleep all day long. Her senses are heightened so certain smells and taste might make her nauseous while hormones rage through her system making mood swings happen with ease - take comfort knowing that morning sickness usually subsides by week 14 which also coincides when most women will have their energy levels completely return back to normal too! Below are some ideas on what you can do during this period:

Antenatal care visits

The care you give your partner during this time will have impacts for years to come. With tight work schedules, I understand that this may be difficullt. But when possible, accompany your partner for her antenatal appointments. Keep close tabs on her progress. Watching your little baby during a scan, kicking away on the screen as you hear the rhythm of his little heartbeat with your the mom can be a wonderful bonding exercise.

Sometimes they seem like unimportant appointments, but there can be moments when she receives unexpected news. You don't want her to be alone during such times. If you can only attend a few, go for the ultrasounds and be sure to call her after all the others to show her you care.

Reading and discussing

It's always a nice way to spend some time together, and you'll both learn more about the process along the way! Keep track of the pregnancy, including creating a scrapbook of different milestones and the feelings felt during pregnancy. Use a journal as a fun way to share special moments. There are also plenty of video resources out there too if reading isn't your thing or it just doesn't fit into your schedule.

Listen and observe.

It is one thing to hear your partner…it is another to listen. Simply listening to how she feels, her fears, her worries, and any of her anxieties about pregnancy is helpful in itself. She knows you don't have all the answers, but she may still need to vent to someone about what she is dealing with.

On a deeper level, do you feel you came away from the conversation with a better understanding of their positioning? Do you feel they came away from it with a better understanding of yours? Do you feel concerns were addressed and a mutual conclusion determined? Did a positive shift occur in you and/or your partner's body language to indicate that the discussion was resolved satisfactorily?

Before moving on another topic of discussion, verify that all parties feel heard. Listen to the words and language used, reflect on the body language exhibited, and welcome any follow-up discussion as needed.

Feeding Her.

Before you go your separate ways for the day, indulge in a nice breakfast together. You can choose to make something at home or go check out a new breakfast eatery in your neighborhood.

Otherwise, you should know that an empty stomach can up the nausea, so make sure she has a healthy snack (trail mix, a granola bar) stashed on the nightstand to nibble on when she wakes up. Everything she's eating, make sure it is healthy, nutritious food that's easy to digest so she can feel her best each day.

If nausea becomes a problem, try making recipes without strong smells or tasting salty and spicy foods.

Lighten Up And Clear The Way.

One way to make the bathroom an easier place for Mom is by installing nightlights. This will help her see better and avoid any accidents on dark pathways at nighttime or in dimly lit hallways. To prevent confusion, it's also important to clear a path from her bedroom door all the way into the main lavatory area so she can easily find it without error when she needs relief during inconvenient hours of day time or night-time.

THE SECOND TRIMESTER: WEEK 14 -27

You know what they say: when it rains, it pours. Your wife's pregnancy has been difficult enough with morning sickness and fatigue. During this time, the morning sickness should be gone, she will have a little more energy and her mood swings are less intense, but now that the second trimester is underway she's experiencing a whole new set of challenges. She'll have trouble sleeping at night because your unborn baby is demanding more space in there, and she may experience heartburn or leg cramps as well! The good news is that you can still do a lot to help your pregnant partner during this time.

Feel Your Baby (On Consent).

Something as subtle and beautiful as a baby's first movements can only be felt by the mother. What does it feel like when you know your unborn child is moving? Incredible!

I remember my own mom telling me about her experience cradling us in utero while she slept on the couch or walked around town shopping for clothes to prepare our arrival into this world. I was very young at the time but still have vivid memories now - how we kicked less often during certain times of day, what positions were best for restful sleep (she always said not too much lying down), which foods helped settle tummy aches after eating.

If you don't want to be left out, then get a front row seat to your baby's performance by placing your hand on her belly. You will be able to tell if the kicks are strong or gentle, and you can also count them! Also, talk/sing to your baby. Hearing your voice helps your baby feel attached to you quickly once he/she is born.

Make Her Sleep Better

Raising your pregnant partner's head and shoulders on a pillow while she sleeps can help alleviate pain in her back or hips.

The benefits of sleeping with the right support include better breathing, which may lessen snoring; relief from acid reflux symptoms like heartburn and nausea that might otherwise keep you up at night; less pressure on joints such as knees and wrists - all thanks to an extra set of hands so one person doesn't have to do it alone!

Give Her a Belly Rub.

Your partner's bump is growing bigger, and so the skin stretches. It can be dryer or itchy as a result of this change in size! Rub shea butter or any other moisturizing creams on her belly to alleviate these issues for your partner. This would also make an excellent way to pamper them if they are feeling uncomfortable with their changing figure while pregnant!

THE THIRD TRIMESTER: WEEK 28 -40

The third trimester is an intense time for pregnant partners. It can be a struggle to help your partner through her discomforts, and she may need more support than ever before! For example, the baby's weight becomes really heavy towards the end of pregnancy; tiredness and irritability often return as well- you might even notice that peeing will become frequent (it won't stop!). Pregnancy brain also occurs during this phase of the pregnancy.

Washroom watchout.

You can prevent a lot of falls and mishaps by installing handrails in the shower. They're inexpensive, easy to install, and will provide your loved one with much more independence when it comes time for them to get out of the bath or adjust their position while bathing. You may also want to roll up area rugs or tape down carpets so that slipping is less likely if they do happen to fall over on these surfaces.

Pack your hospital bag.

Your bag is just as important as hers. You should have your bag packed by week 36 because babies don't always come on schedule. Bring a change of clothes, toothbrush and toothpaste, snacks and drinks, something to keep you occupied, digital camera and most importantly your mobile phone and all other dad's survival kit.

Disconnect to connect.

Schedule some time together during the week and turn off your phone, tablet, and other devices. When you do so, you are making a conscious decision to connect with your partner. You are prioritizing time with your partner over checking out the newest posts on social media, giving your relationship a much-needed boost. Want to make it extra special? Talk about why you love your partner and what you are looking forward to as you welcome your new baby.

Sieze the baby-less moments

Let's face it - errand runs are monotonous and we often dread carving out time to get them done during the week. Why not ask for a little company to make the experience more enjoyable? Have a grocery list that must be tackled? Do it together. Need to pick up her prescription? Turn it into an outing. Got a gift that you need to mail for your best friend's birthday? Grab your partner's hand and head to the post office. Going on errand runs together gives you an opportunity to steal moments throughout the week. It's a chance to catch up on what you both have done during the week and what you are looking forward to next week.

Write love notes.

We are taking this old-school! Plan an activity where you exchange love notes every day during a designated time. Maybe you want to do it in your third trimester as you prepare for two to become one. Grab a post-it note and a pen and write a sweet message to your partner. Your partner should do the same. At the beginning of every day during this designated time, exchange your written love notes but do not open them right then and there. Open them later in the day when you are apart. You and your partner can talk about what the notes meant to you after you have finally opened them. Save them to a scrapbook if you wish to preserve them.

Install your baby's car seat.

you can't drive home from the hospital without a car seat and they can be complicated to install, so don't wait till the very last minute. If you're having trouble, get help from an authorised restraint fitting station.

Fill up the freezer.

Save your future self some serious kitchen time by stocking up the freezer with healthy meals before the arrival of your baby. It's a major stress reliever not having to prepare meals in the first 2 weeks if you do not have family around to cook for you.

OTHER WAYS YOU CAN SUPPORT YOUR PARTNER

Compliment her.

Your partner's body is going to change during pregnancy and there is no way to avoid that. She may struggle with this and she may be fine and embrace it. Regardless, compliment your bunny often. Tell her how pretty she looks, how she is glowing, or how happy she has seemed lately in her element of baby planning. Whatever it may be, do not underestimate how important it is to compliment your partner.

Don't comment on the nesting.

You may wonder who came in and replaced your once normal partner with this woman whose idea of fun is cleaning baseboards and the inside of the dishwasher on a Friday night but just go with it. supporting mom-to-be during pregnancy sometimes just means you let her nest. Nesting, aka cleaning and preparing for the baby, is a normal part of pregnancy. Just roll with it because you'll have a cleaner house because of it! If you're feeling like you can keep up with her cleaning frenzy, offer to pitch in!

Be enthusiastic about the birthing classes.

Birthing classes don't exactly sound like something you'd want to sign up for or get excited about but don't make too many complaints about this. Childbirth is already something she has to undergo herself and she may be very nervous about it. Do your best to be supportive and enthusiastic about any class that is going to help put your partner's mind at ease–you may even learn something yourself!

Allow her some "me time".

Arrange for a night where you leave the (already clean!) house for her so she can simply relax with some peace. Encourage her to go to a spa or get her nails done. As much as she loves you, sometimes the hormones she's dealing with leave her feeling too tired to even interact. So watch out for these moments and let her know your planning to get out of her hair for just a few hours so she can do whatever she wants!

Do the dishes.

Or the laundry…or the vacuuming…you get the idea. Anything you think you can do to help out around the house will be much appreciated by your tired consort who is working harder than she even realizes to grow a new baby. After a long day dealing with a changing body and hormones, even the smallest household chores can feel like a mountain to a pregnant woman. So keep an eye out for those little things!

Indulge on occasion.

Your partner may be trying her best to stay active and healthy during her pregnancy, but there are always those few occasions where a craving just needs to be satisfied. Humor her and enjoy running out for milkshakes together. It will make her feel better and at least you can share these moments. You probably don't want to fully gain sympathy weight, but if you do, at least you are in it together!

Bond over hobbies and interests.

If you have an interest in a particular topic or activity, share with your partner. For example, if you love history documentaries and notice an interesting one that is premiering next week, turn it to a movie night. It's okay if she doesn't like it. Understand that she can be moody or have preference. If possible, opt for her choices. Be open to your partner if they make the same request. When couples connect through a passion, it can lead to a deeper intimacy. For example, if your partner enjoys completing puzzles, ask if you can join them. Working together towards a common goal can lead to feelings of fondness and mutual respect.

Have in-depth conversations about parenting.

Now is a great time to talk about your excitement and concerns about the future. Consider talking about how you might want to parent - maybe you are considering an authoritarian parenting style while your partner is leaning more towards an authoritative parenting style. Or maybe you find attachment parenting concepts interesting, like co-sleeping, while your partner is envisioning that your child will sleep in their own room after birth. Either way, you can intimately connect with your partner by talking about how you hope to parent collaboratively and effectively. You do not have to have it all figured out today, tomorrow, or next month, but this conversation can provide good food for thought as you walk into this next stage.

Talk baby.

It can feel like your to-do list is never-ending when you are supporting your partner during pregnancy. From baby names to nursery themes to finding the right pediatrician, you may find yourself overwhelmed by the sheer number of things that must be done before your little one comes home. Sit down and write out what you hope to accomplish before that point. Talk about things that you are both excited and concerned about as you tackle this list. During these conversations, you may talk about who the baby might look like or whose personality they will have. She may discover that you are nervous about diapering the baby properly while you may confide that you worry about how to get the baby settled into a routine. Once you have these excitements and concerns out in the open, this is a chance to really bond.

Be honest.

During this time, you may feel a lot of emotions, some positive and some negative. Discuss them as they come up so you and your partner are on the same page. If you have a concern about something your partner has or has not done, talk about it up in a way that you are focused on finding a solution to the problem. By focusing on a solution to the problem, why the solution is necessary, and not your partner specifically, you can acknowledge what is upsetting you while also making steps to move forward in a constructive way.

4

THE P'S AND Q'S OF PREGNANCY

"It is better to be safe than sorry"

— SAMUEL LOVER

You already know that before your little bundle of joy arrives, you and mama are responsible for helping them grow in a nurturing, healthy environment.

This probably leaves you with a lot of questions and worries about possibilities; from what your woman can eat, to the foods she should avoid, whether she can keep on with her exercise, and how to have sex again.

While you can't prevent every possible complication, I will share with you a list of what to do and what to avoid during pregnancy to help reduce pregnancy complications and keep your baby healthy.

HAVE SEX IF SHE'S UP FOR IT

Sex is an essential part of a healthy relationship, and pregnancy does not have to put a damper on your sex life. You may be wondering if it is safe to have sex during pregnancy or if you will hurt the baby by having intercourse. The answer is no! Unless your partner's health care provider has told her otherwise, you can have sex throughout the entire 9 months. Sex is not harmful because the baby is protected within the uterus and cushioned by fluid.

Besides your doctor's warnings, there are also other situations when you could not have sex with your pregnant partner.

While these are basically commonsensical considerations, it remains practical to still point the obvious, such as:

- Having a history of miscarriage or premature birth
- The placenta is covering the cervix (this is Placenta previa in medical terms)
- Her water has broken
- She is having bleeding problems
- Your (or your partner's) religious belief or cultural upbringing about pregnancy sex (if ever there is such a thing)
- Either you, or your partner, has sexually-transmitted disease (told you, these are obvious considerations).

SOME SEX POSITIONS YOU COULD TRY:

Wife on top

While some men may complain that they feel helpless when the woman is on top and is the one in control, this position works best during pregnancy as your wife can control how deep you penetrate inside her. She is also in control of how fast or slow the session will be.

On all-fours

This is sometimes referred to as"doggy-style." At the early stages of pregnancy, this could actually be one of the most preferred positions. The wife does not have to exert much effort and there is no direct pressure on the tummy. However, when the belly becomes bigger, it would be heavier and it might get pressed against the bed or pressed between her legs and upper torso. As long as she could keep her belly raised, this would work as just one of those position for a shorter time before switching to another position.

Spooning

This could be one of the most erotic and sensual positions lovers could have. The woman sits in front of the man who is also in a seated position. There is no pressure on the stomach, and the man could reach in front for added stimulation to his partner's erogenous zones.

Lying on one side

This position frees the woman's back from pressure, and the tummy is safely supported by its side. With one leg raise, the man could enter from either behind or he can be position perpendicularly (like a letter "T" position) and penetrate while facing her. This could be a tricky position at first but once you get the hang of it, you'd find that this is less strenuous for both of you.

If, for some reasons, you can't do any of the above, the simple but very intimate mutual stimulation of the partner's sex organ would do the trick.

IF SHE'S NOT UP FOR SEX:

Talk.

Maybe your partner wants other intimate gestures, like kissing and cuddling, more than sex. That's okay! Like I said, your partner's desire for intimacy and sex in general can shift during pregnancy. With all of the changes that are happening to her, she may not be as interested in the sex life as she used to be in the past.

Sit down and talk about it to get ahead of any incompatibility issues that may arise going forward. If you are unsure how to communicate what you are feeling and need insight into how to communicate, consult with a therapist who specializes in families and relationships for help finding the right words.

Hug it out.

Embrace your partner when you can and enjoy the feeling. You don't have to talk or escalate to anything more if your partner does not want to do so. Hugs, and other intimate acts like kissing and sex, cause our body to release oxytocin. Oxytocin is also known as the "cuddle" or "love hormone". Not only is a nice, cozy, and long hug a great way to get closer to your partner, it is also reduces your anxiety levels. So reach for your partner and encourage them to do the same!

Indulge in a DIY couples' massage.

Grab a luxurious bottle of massage oil, dim the lights, lay down, and take turns massaging each other. This intimate act is a wonderful way to connect physically without having sex. If you want to emulate a spa setting, you and your partner can turn on some soft jazz, put a few drops of lavender oil in an oil diffuser, and set up nice, soft sheets on your bed. Focus on keeping the massage loving and slow for the ultimate evening. Want to make the DIY massage extra special? Light candles, or better yet, use battery-operated tea lights. If you want to use candles, just remember to keep an eye on them and blow out when you are done.

INDULGE IN EXERCISE

Staying active during pregnancy is important for expecting moms. The various benefits of simple exercises during pregnancy include pain management, mood regulation, better sleep, and preventing excessive weight gain. In addition, a small new study showed that prenatal aerobic exercises could lead to healthier weight in babies. Of course, it goes without saying that doctors should be consulted before undertaking any workout routine to prevent untoward incidents.

They have to be careful not to do anything that's too strenuous, gets their heart rate up too high or increases their body temperature too much. Below are a number of workouts you and your partner can do that won't overstress the already-sore joints.

Yoga

Prenatal yoga can help a mom-to-be deal with the changes her body endures during pregnancy notes the American Pregnancy Association (APA). The poses are designed to increase flexibility and strengthen muscles while helping to develop breathing and relaxation techniques that could help a woman get through labor.

It can also include improved sleep along with decreased lower back pain, nausea and headaches while also reducing the chance of preterm labor.

Hot or Bikram yoga are not recommended for pregnant women due to the hot environment class is conducted in.

Stationary Bikes

Like swimming, bicycling is one exercise that doesn't cause unnecessary body stress, since the bike supports the woman's weight according to the APA. The risk of falling is also reduced when biking. And, it's a year-round exercise since, most gyms have stationary bikes.

Intense spin classes, however, are not recommended for pregnant women, since they can get pretty hot and raise your heart rate.

Walking

Don't underestimate how beneficial walking can be. It's easy to work into your schedule and doesn't take a toll on your knees like running can. Be sure to wear comfortable shoes, notes the APA, while setting realistic distance goals.

Swimming

Hop in the pool with your partner and give swimming a shot. Swimming provides an overall body workout without putting stress on joints. It also helps raise the heart rate without the risk of overheating.

A swim is also a good way to cool down if her third trimester happens to be during the hot summer months.

HELP MAMA GRAB SOME SLEEP

According to "science," if you live for 75 years, you will spend 25 of those years asleep. Unless you have a pregnant partner at any time during those 75 years, in which case you will actually sleep for 24 years and 3 months. But, wait, that actually probably doesn't account for after the baby is born, so subtract at least another 3 years. Oh, and then they'll be reckless teenagers, so maybe shave off another 4 years. You know what? Forget it. Who needs sleep anyway?

Well, actually, your pregnant partner needs sleep. But it turns out that growing a human is pretty restless work. Luckily, there are some things you can do to help her get some shut eye, none of which include telling her your boring theories about the MLB post-season. Though that might work too.

Help Her Keep A Schedule

After having the baby, you'll learn quickly that sticking to a strict schedule is crucial for getting your kid to sleep. So you might as well start practicing with your partner now, because it turns out a regular sleep schedule will help her too.

So when bedtime rolls around, maybe try not to pressure her into just one more episode of Narcos. But feel free to skip the lullabye and the reading of Goodnight Moon.

Help Her Reduce Anxiety

She might already be into yoga and mindfulness meditations, which'll help her de-stress. But you have something that she hasn't got: some strong magic fingers (and they're 'uge so guaranteed no problem there). What are they good for? Some good old-fashioned prenatal-massage.

Beyond that? Try not to talk about nervous-making baby issues before bed. Topics like what to expect from prenatal testing a best left for the morning, much like high fiber cereals.

Help Her With The Meals

Cooking can be a hassle. If you're tired from a whole day of gestating, it can be tough thinking about digestion. Which can lead to processed meals and indigestion. That's no good for sleepy times.

So go ahead and man the stove, man. Try some non-spicy recipes that avoid anything that requires being submerged in hot fat — bonus points for some added folic acid. You can sneak in some wings when you're out with your bros, but making some good meals for her now will help her heart burn only for you.

Deal With Your Snoring

Your nighttime breathing exploits sound like a dog fight. That's not only disturbing, it's downright unethical. If there was ever a time to fix your ridiculous schnoz-racket, it's before sleep gets really dicey in the third trimester.

Try elevating the head of the bed (which might help her too) or using those nasal strips. If things are truly jacked, get your doc to hook you up with a self-administered at-home sleep study and go from there.

THINGS TO AVOID (THE DON'TS OF PREGNANCY)

Undercooked, Raw, And Processed Meats

You might have heard that pregnant women should avoid deli meats, and that's true! That's because deli meat (and lunch meat, hotdogs, and other processed meats) can become contaminated with bacteria during processing, packaging, or storage. These bacteria can threaten her health.

In addition, bacteria can lead to serious health problems for your baby, including severe neurological illnesses (like blindness, epilepsy, or intellectual disability). In extreme cases, these bacteria can even cause stillbirth.

To ensure both mom and baby are safe from these dangerous bacteria – such as E. coli, Salmonella, Listeria, and Toxoplasma, you should encourage mama to stop eating undercooked or raw meat during pregnancy. It's best to make sure the meat is completely cooked through.

Alcohol

Pregnant women are strongly urged not to drink alcohol during pregnancy. This substance can cause many complications during pregnancy, have damaging effects on developing fetus, and may contribute to other medical problems as your child grows.

When a pregnant woman drinks alcohol, it travels through her bloodstream and into the fetus. That means that when mom has a glass of wine, your baby has a glass of wine, too. In addition, drinking alcohol can lead to eating less, thus losing sources of nutrients.

Furthermore, alcohol consumption during pregnancy can cause what is known as fetal alcohol syndrome (FAS). FAS includes mental and physical birth defects and growth problems associated with the mother's high levels of alcohol use during pregnancy.

Smoking

The same rule applies to smoking. Smoking is dangerous to your baby during and after pregnancy, and makes it harder for mom to recover from delivery. Smoking deprives the fetus of oxygen, which can also lead to accelerated ovarian aging; a higher risk of miscarriage, and low birth weight babies.

What's more? Once your baby is born, there is a higher likelihood of the child having developmental issues like mental and behavioral problems.

Fresh-squeezed Juice

Pregnant women should opt for juice that is pasteurized. Fresh-squeezed juice in restaurants, juice bars, or farm stands may not be pasteurized to protect against harmful bacteria, including salmonella and E. coli. Some markets also sell raw, unpasteurized juice in the refrigerated case — look for the required warning label, and steer clear. Juice in boxes and bottles on your supermarket shelf is also safe.

Raw Eggs

Raw eggs or any foods that contain raw eggs should be avoided because of the potential exposure to salmonella. Some homemade Caesar dressings, mayonnaise, homemade ice cream or custards, and Hollandaise sauces may be made with raw eggs. If the recipe is cooked at some point, this will reduce the exposure to salmonella. Commercially manufactured ice cream, dressings, and eggnog is made with pasteurized eggs and do not increase the risk of salmonella. Sorry, but you should probably resist the raw cookie dough too if it contains raw eggs.

Restaurants should be using pasteurized eggs in any recipe that is made with raw eggs, such as Hollandaise sauce or dressings.

Soft Cheeses

Imported soft cheeses may contain listeria bacteria. It's best to avoid soft cheeses such as Brie, Camembert, Roquefort, Feta, Gorgonzola, and Mexican style cheeses that include Queso Blanco and Queso Fresco unless they clearly state that they are made from pasteurized milk. All soft non-imported cheeses made with pasteurized milk are safe to eat.

Caffeine

Although most studies show that caffeine intake in moderation is permissible, there are others that show that caffeine intake may be related to miscarriages. Encourage mom to avoid caffeine during the first trimester to reduce the likelihood of a miscarriage. As a general rule, caffeine should be limited to fewer than 200 mg per day during pregnancy. That's one 12-ounce cup of coffee. Caffeine is a diuretic, which means it helps eliminate fluids from the body. Don't forget, her favorite soda, chocolate or energy drink probably contains caffeine too.

This can result in water and calcium loss. It is important that your woman is drinking plenty of water, juice, and milk rather than caffeinated beverages. Some research shows that large amounts of caffeine are associated with miscarriage, premature birth, low birth weight, and withdrawal symptoms in infants. The safest thing is to refrain from consuming caffeine.

5

THE NEW DAD CHEATSHEET

"Always plan ahead. It wasn't raining when Noah built the Ark."

— RICHARD CUSHING.

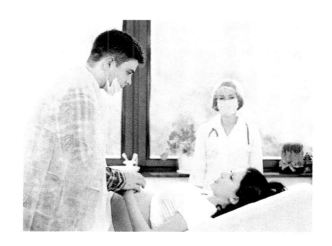

I f you've never been in a delivery room before, you may feel uncertain about your job. Are you supposed to be a cheerleader, a coach, or an unofficial nurse? It's usually a little bit of everything. Your partner will need you at every stage, from the first contractions to the delivery and beyond. You can prepare ahead of time by taking a birthing class with her or talking to other dads about the experience.

One of the best ways to prepare for childbirth is to accompany your partner to a childbirth education class. Almost all hospitals and birth centers hold classes, and parents-to-be are usually given the option of attending two or three short evening sessions or one long daytime session. You can also choose to go to an offsite class, where the focus may be more on natural childbirth.

Before taking a class, it helps to know a little about childbirth. Here are some of the things you may learn and discuss in a childbirth class:

RECOGNIZING THE ONSET OF TRUE LABOR

Late in pregnancy, many women have painful contractions that may feel like false labor – Braxton Hicks contractions that may start strong but taper off and then stop after a while. Look for these signs, among others, that your partner is experiencing the real deal:

Her water may break, resulting in a trickle or a gush of fluid. When the amniotic sac (also called the bag of waters) breaks, many women spontaneously go into labor shortly after. If not, labor is often induced to minimize the risk of developing an infection. But keep in mind that contractions usually start before her water breaks.

Persistent lower back pain, especially if your partner also complains about a crampy, premenstrual feeling.

Contractions that occur at regular and increasingly shorter intervals and become longer and stronger in intensity.

She passes the mucus plug, which is in the cervix. This isn't necessarily a sign that labor is imminent – it could still be several days away. But at the very least, it indicates that things are moving along.

TIMING THE CONTRACTIONS

Use a timer – for most people, this will be the one on their phone, but anything that will count seconds is fine – to time your partner's contractions in seconds from the beginning of one contraction to the beginning of the next. Count the frequency of contractions in minutes.

If she's having regular painful contractions lasting 30 seconds or more, she's probably in early labor. Your doctor or midwife can help you decide on the phone about when to come in.

As a general rule, if the contractions are five minutes apart or less, last more than 30 seconds, and continue in that pattern for an hour, it's time to go to the hospital. Some situations call for getting to the hospital sooner, so talk to your caregiver ahead of time about what's right for you.

HECK! IT'S TIME FOR HOSPITAL

Don't head to the hospital the minute your partner goes into labor. If she's dilated to only 1 centimeter, chances are they'll send you home or tell her to go for a walk until it's clear she's in labor.

Take a walk, go to the mall or a museum, hit the beach, catch a movie – do anything to help your partner take her mind off the contractions. Though it may not be easy, try not to fixate on the clock. If labor begins at night, help your partner get back to sleep for a few hours.

KNOW WHAT TO EXPECT DURING LABOR

Forget those TV sitcom episodes in which a woman goes into labor and a baby pops out by the second commercial. It sometimes happens that fast, but not usually. For most women, especially first-time mothers, labor is a journey, not an event.

Don't expect labor to be over in just a few hours. Every woman's experience is different, but it's helpful to understand that there are three distinct stages of labor:

FIRST STAGE OF LABOR

The first stage consists of three phases:

Early phase: This phase typically lasts up to 12 hours although it's usually considerably shorter for second and subsequent babies. As labor progresses, the contractions get longer and stronger.

Active phase: Often this phase lasts up to six hours, although it can be a lot shorter. You should be in the hospital or birth center by now or en route. Contractions are much more intense, last about 40 to 60 seconds, and are spaced three to five minutes apart.

Breathing exercises, relaxation techniques, and coaching are all important now. If your partner is having trouble coping or she's not interested in drug-free labor, this is when she might opt for an epidural or other pain relief.

Transition phase: This phase can last anywhere from a few minutes to several hours. It's here that your partner is most likely to swear at you like a truck driver. (Don't take it personally – even women who have coped well up to this point often "lose it" during the transition phase.)

Contractions last 40 to 60 seconds and come two or three minutes apart.

SECOND STAGE OF LABOR

Pushing and birth. The second stage can last from minutes to hours – the average is about an hour for a first-time pregnancy (longer if she's had an epidural) – and ends with a moment that's made up in equal parts of relief and breathtaking beauty: The birth of your baby.

There's a lot to think about during this phase: Do you want to record the birth on video? Will you want to cut the cord? (Be sure to remind your doctor or midwife if you do and be aware that some hospitals don't allow pictures or videos in the birthing room.)

Does your partner want to try to breastfeed immediately after birth? If so, be sure to tell your doctor and nurses so they can help with that as soon as it's safe for your baby to do so.

THIRD STAGE

Delivery of the placenta. It's not over yet! This stage, which begins immediately after the birth of your baby and ends with the delivery of the placenta five to 10 minutes later, is usually anticlimactic but necessary.

Your partner may get a case of chills or feel very shaky during this phase. If that's the case, be ready to offer a warm blanket and to hold your newborn while your partner's regaining her strength.

"WHAT'S MY JOB, ANYWAY?"

Above all, you should ask your partner to talk about what she wants and needs. She'll let you know. It's a good idea to discuss with her what she thinks she'll want from you during labor. It should be your job to make all the arrangements for getting to the hospital. You should also be the one to keep in touch with the rest of the family and screen phone calls while labor is in progress.

Early labor

During the first few hours of labor, your main job is to be a distraction. Ask her if she wants her back or feet rubbed. Put on some music and walk around the room with her. Encourage her to do anything other than lying still and dreading the next contraction.

Active labor

As contractions become stronger and closer together, your role becomes more and more important. If you attended a birthing class, now's the time to put all of those lessons into action. If you didn't go to a class, ask the nurse for tips.

At this point, your main job is to help keep your partner focused. She shouldn't give up, and she shouldn't panic. If she starts acting restless or agitated during a contraction, make eye contact with her and encourage her to take a deep breath. Hold her hand and tell her she's doing great.

But be prepared for the possibility that your encouragement may not be well received at times. One San Francisco doctor recalls a dad whose wife screamed at him to shut up when he told her -- in mid-contraction -- that she was doing great. Between contractions, you will be your partner's caretaker and servant at the same time. If she wants some ice chips, you'll be getting some. Pronto. If she wants a back rub, you'll be rolling up your sleeves and getting to work.

Delivery

This is the big moment, an event you'll remember for the rest of your life. And here's the tough part: You must STAY CALM. Try to save your tears and hysteria until after the baby is born. Your wife needs your support, figuratively and literally. You'll be giving her encouragement with every push, and you may also be supporting her back so she can push comfortably. If you're up to it, you should also take a few moments to watch the actual birth. When you get your first glimpse of your baby's head, you can reassure your partner that she's almost done.

The Aftermath

Men often have two impulses after watching their child being born. First, they cry. Then they grab a camera. As your partner holds your baby for the first time, you'll be firing the flashbulb. After a few good shots, you'll want to put down the camera and pick up your baby. Hold him close and let him study your face.

If your baby goes to a nursery while your partner recovers, go along and keep him company. When he drifts off to sleep, you can make the first round of phone calls to friends and family. And don't forget to check in with your partner, too. If she's awake, she'll want to hear the very latest on the baby's condition. She'll also want to hear how great she was.

Cut The Cord if You Want

Many dads and partners choose to cut their baby's umbilical cord in the first minutes after birth. If you want to cut the cord, don't be shy about reminding your partner's doctor or midwife.

When The Unexpected Happens

You and your wife should already have a detailed birth plan. You should know what kind of interventions she wants or doesn't want, and you should be ready to remind doctors and nurses of her wishes. But once labor starts, you have to be prepared for the unexpected. If the labor isn't going smoothly, your wife might need an intervention that she hadn't signed up for, such as pain medication or even a cesarean section.

If there's a decision to be made, your cool head will be essential in helping her make it. And when your child asks about his birthday, you'll have a story to tell.

TRANSITION WITH BABY FROM HOSPITAL TO HOME

It's time to make your great escape back home with your baby, you may think it's as simple as going from A to B. After all, you've done the drive a fair few times. A couple of days ago, in fact. But oh no. It's not as simple as grab-and-go. Because once it's time to bring baby home, you ignite the dad-mode of travel. So what can new parents, expect?

Whether your baby comes home from the hospital right away, arrives later (perhaps after a stay in the neonatal intensive care unit), or comes through an adoption agency, the homecoming of your little one is a major event you've probably often imagined. It is a momentous journey that you'll remember forever. Behold my handy guide to bringing your baby home from the hospital in these easy steps.

Discharge and paperwork.

Before you can go, the midwife needs to discharge you. The baby needs a last looking over. And you will probably stand thisclose to the doctor to make sure everything is okay.

Get bub ready to go.

Dress your newborn and gently place them into the capsule (or in your arms if you're using a non-transferable car seat).

Take a picture of bub in a capsule.

Naw… Your little one is so small in that big car seat. And so squishy. Take 15 different pictures, just to make sure you get the right angle.

Realize bub has pooed.

He has pooed all over that super-cute 'going-home' outfit. And, if you're (un)lucky, it's leached through to the car seat too. Take baby out. Retrieve emergency going-home outfit out of the bag and redress bub. Repeat step three.

Stop.

Let every person coo over your newborn as you walk through the ward. Because no one can resist having a sneaky peek at a brand new baby in a capsule. And how can you resist not wanting to share all that royal squishiness with all those new admirers?

Exit the hospital.

Fresh air! Glorious fresh air! This is probably the first time your newborn has been exposed to outdoor air. So naturally, you're going to freak out that their head is cold and frantically pull the nappy bag apart to search for the itty bitty baby beanie.

Put baby into the car seat.

This is usually the time when new parents discover that the whiz-bang car seat they religiously road-tested doesn't click in and out so easily when an actual baby is inside. Try 87 times. Finally, get it.

Once you have bub clipped in and ready to go, expect to check that they are safe and secure another 35 times. This average goes down dramatically with each subsequent child.

Return to hospital.

Because you're pretty sure you left the baby's dummy on the counter. And possibly part of your mind too. Retrieve the dummy. Realize that your partner's pre-baby brain won't be returning anytime soon.

Take more photos of baby in capsule.

#babysfirstdrive #supercuteness #slowdown

Get the trek home.

You're on the road. And in the middle of crazy rush-hour traf-fic. As bub is now asleep you have nothing to focus on except the dangers all around you. Buses, trucks, Deliveroo drivers.

And naturally, it's your fault (according to mom) for taking this route.

Enter house.

And a brand new wild journey ahead. Sure, the house might look the same as when you left it, but the world will never be the same again after bringing home baby. Buckle up! The car ride home is just the beginning.

SETTLING IN COMFORTABLY AFTER THE TRANSITION

It's okay to be nervous when bringing baby home from the hospital, especially if this is your first child. It's also completely normal to feel uncertain or even overwhelmed as you and your newborn discover sleeping and feeding routines that work best.

However, if overwhelmed feelings worsen or develop into feelings of depression, hopelessness, or despair, contact your healthcare provider right away. There's no shame in doing so. Many parents don't realize that their hormones are likely to continue shifting for months after giving birth, which can also contribute to what may feel like a roller-coaster of emotions.

As you transition from hospital to home, decide how and when you'd like family, friends, and other visitors to stop by. It's perfectly acceptable to ask anyone who was recently under the weather to wait until they're feeling 100% well before coming over to visit you or the baby.

You may also consider asking visitors to wash their hands before helping with or holding your little one since his or her immune system is still very immature and continues to develop after birth before being at full strength.

Most importantly, it's essential to remember to go with the flow during your newborn's first few weeks and months at home – whether you are experiencing motherhood for the first time or you have other children. Your family just got bigger and it may take some time to get back into routines (or even get a full night of sleep!), but these are precious moments that won't last forever and should ultimately be enjoyed.

WHEN TO CALL THE DOCTOR

Your baby's health care provider expects calls from new parents on many topics, including breastfeeding and health concerns (for more on newborn care, visit the Pregnancy & Newborns section). They'd rather have you call than worry about something needlessly.

If you wonder whether you should call the doctor's office, do it, especially if you see something unexpected or different that concerns you. Call if you see any of these signs:

- Rectal temperature of 100.4°F (38°C) or higher (in babies younger than 2 months)
- Symptoms of dehydration (crying without tears, sunken eyes, a depression in the soft spot on baby's head, no wet diapers in 6 to 8 hours)
- A soft spot that bulges when your baby's quiet and upright
- A baby that is difficult to rouse
- Rapid or labored breathing (call 911 if your baby has breathing difficulty and begins turning bluish around the lips or mouth)
- Repeated forceful vomiting or an inability to keep fluids down
- Bloody vomit or stool
- More than eight diarrhea stools in 8 hours.

6

NEW DAD SURVIVAL KIT

"Getting organized is a sign of self-respect."

— GABRIELLE BERNSTEIN

Have you ever heard your dad talk about the day you were born? He may be able to describe the weather or the big story on the television news. Chances are, though, he can't talk about your actual birth. Back then, fathers were often barred from the delivery room. While your mother was pushing, your dad was probably in another room, worrying and looking at his watch.

When you talk to your kids, the story will be different. You'll be able to describe the look on their faces when they entered the world. You'll be able to tell them how you felt watching them being born. And you'll be able to recount their mom's heroism. She did all the hard work, but you were right beside her. And that's pretty heroic, too.

Waiting for the birth of a new baby, and expecting it anytime in the last months of pregnancy is not an easy experience at all. The last few months of pregnancy passed very slow and heavy on both of us; me and my wife.

One day my wife felt some real pain, we hurried to the hospital, the doctor made a quick check and it was a false alarm! The baby was training us on how to respond to the event. He was checking whether we were ready or not? He was testing the speed of our response and all the precautions we were preparing. It was not funny when it happened, but after it passed, we were more mature towards the false alarms!

A few days later, the alarm was not false and that's how my journey to "BECOMING A FATHER" began.

When it's your turn, it's likely to happen when you least expect it. And if you don't get some things in place now, then I'm sorry... you may love neither yourself nor the experience that day.

The word NO

Trust me on this one, after having three kids you need to learn when it comes birthing time to use the word no. Remember you are trying to keep your partner comfortable during the process and she may not want those visitors peaking in. So you have to step in and say no. At times it may not be no but you may need to redirect with, can you come back in 30 minutes as my wife is feeding the baby or resting, etc. If you have a tough time saying no then start practicing once you find out you're having a kid, as there will be some point during the delivery process you will have to say no to someone.

Snacks

Since this is your first time in the hospital awaiting the arrival of your baby then you might notice that sometimes time seems to stand still. While you are doing great at encouraging your partner, your stomach is probably saying "Hey, don't forget about me!". It is important to grab some snacks to help you keep up the energy you will need during labor and then delivery! Pick some great treats high in protein like peanut butter crackers, protein bars, or your favorite candy! Just make sure the smell won't be offensive to your laboring partner. We learned our lessons, that's why we are writing this new dad hospital survival kit

Pain Relievers

While you might be up on your feet and running around making sure your partner is stocked with ice chips, cool cloths, laboring balls, and everything else in between you might just notice that your feet are getting sore. Since you are packing your own bag for the hospital go ahead and throw in some Tylenol or Ibuprofen. Those will come in handy when your back, feet, or head begin to hurt from running around or sleeping on those uncomfortable Hospital couches. No mom wants to hear you complain about pain during this time! Take it from me, I am here to help you out!

Change of clothes

As your mom-to-be is preparing and planning for the new baby to arrive by packing all the essentials that she and your newborn will need sometimes they often overlook dads. To make sure she did not pick out matching outfits, go ahead and pack a couple of days worth of clothes. Comfy clothes to lounge around in are great plus a good outfit to go home in!

Phone Chargers or Battery packs

You know everyone and their mother will be blowing up your phone wanting updates on the progress of your partner and baby. You will be like the paparazzi taking a million pictures of the world's most adorable baby. So for WWIII not to start up in the hospital room, you might want to pack a charger or battery pack. I suggest bringing 2 chargers and a fully charged battery pack. Make sure the battery pack is fully charged as nothing like it being dead when you need it. You will thank us later!

Get your Lady a Present

I am not really sure if this is a thing or not but it is better to be prepared than not. You're probably thinking, "Why do I need to give her a present?". Just do it and thank me later. This present is called a Push Gift and it's your gift of gratitude for delivering your baby. It can be, no, it must be something personal and meaningful. So don't get her favorite candy, please. I got my wife a simple necklace with the baby's initials on it! IF you forget the Hospital gift shops have stepped up their game and grab one last minute if you need to but I do suggest getting her something thoughtful.

Toiletries

Dad, if you are going to be at the hospital for a few days then you are going to need to pack a few toiletries. What to include but not limited to these items; soap, shampoo, deodorant, Poo Pourri spray (you're welcome), body wash, razor, and shaving cream. I am sure you will think of some things you will need also based on your personal preferences. But trust me on this one your Queen's senses will be heightened so get some Poo Pourri spray or consider using the public restroom.

Money

Maybe you opted to skip on number two earlier, if so then you will need money for the vending machines. Some hospitals have pay-by-the-hour parking meters so make sure that sucker stays fed. Nothing says congratulations on your new bundle of joy quite like a $200 parking ticket! YIKES!

Instant Coffee

This one is so important on our new dad hospital survival kit that it gets its own slot in this list. I don't know about you but I am a coffee drinker and will need some caffeine while waiting oh so patiently for my newborn to make its appearance! Stay awake and alert while tending to your lady as well! Go ahead and throw in a few others for when that babe is in your arms and your partner is demanding caffeine since she's probably been limited or off caffeine for 9 months! Everyone is happy when mama is happy, right?!

New Dad Shirt

Show off how proud you are of your new addition with a fun new dad shirt! There are tons to choose from and it will probably be better than your old college jersey that has seen better days! Impress your lady with a new shirt!

Entertainment

Even though your main job in the hospital is to help out and assist your partner when needed, there will be some downtime too! She will rest when she can so during that time you will have to entertain yourself. Electronics like our phones, laptops, or even a Nintendo Switch seem to be the easiest and most convenient. Just make sure you don't want to get carried away with the video game or TV show and you start yelling. The other patients just might think you are the one having the baby! Stick to a book, trust me!

Gas Mask

To help lighten the mood and bring a little humor to the room make sure to pack a gas mask. Once your newborn is here and cleaned up, the belly of milk, and all snuggly warm they will poop. Offer to change the diaper but grab the gas mask or dust mask! Being able to bring a little humor to the table as a parent will help you out in the long run. Enjoy the little things! Keep reading for more great things to put in your new dad's hospital survival kit.

Pillow and Blanket

No this is not for your new baby, this is for you! Just like hotels, hospitals are not famous for their soft pillow and blankets.

Bring the comforts of home to help you rest better and not look like a walking zombie for the first few days as you adjust to being a dad. Just make sure the pillowcase and blanket are clean as you don't want the hospital staff to see your sweat stains!

Everyone Say Cheese!

One of the most common things to pack but often time gets overlooked due to the fact that technology has infiltrated our beings is a camera! I know we all have cameras on our phones, but I like to pack an extra camera for those special moments as our cameras don't always take great photos in lower light. As a bonus tip, ask a close friend or relative to be the photographer when you plan to have visitors. This way you can focus on your little one and the guests! There is going to be a lot going on and you might forget to snap a picture of some people. Delegate that to them instead, it will make your life easier!

BABY REGISTRY - MUST-HAVE ITEMS

It's fun to imagine all the cute clothes and adorable toys you want to add to your baby registry, but when it comes to knowing exactly what you need, it can seem daunting. But don't' fret! I have compiled a list of must have baby registry items so you won't be caught unprepared when your little one, or ones, arrive.

Baby clothes

- 6-10 onesies
- 6-10 undershirts
- 5-7 one-piece pajamas
- 1-3 sweaters or jackets
- 1-3 rompers or other dress-up outfits
- 6-8 socks or booties
- 1-3 hats (broad-brimmed for summer, soft cap that covers ears for winter)
- No-scratch mittens
- 3-5 pairs of pants
- 4-6 swaddle blankets
- 2 blanket sleepers for a winter baby
- Bunting bag or fleece suit for a winter baby
- Gentle laundry detergent

Diapering

- Diaper pail and liners
- Diaper bag
- Diaper cream
- Unscented baby wipes (causes less irritation)
- Soft washcloths
- 6-10 dozen cloth diapers and 6-8 diaper covers, or 2-3 large boxes of disposable newborn-size diapers

Baby bedding

- 1-3 washable crib mattress pads
- 2-4 fitted crib sheets
- 4-6 soft, light receiving blankets
- 1-2 heavier blankets for colder climates

Nursery

- Crib, cradle or bassinet
- Firm, flat mattress that fits snugly in crib
- Rocking, glider, or arm chair
- Baby monitor
- Nightlight
- Dresser
- Toy basket
- 3-4 learning activity toys
- 3-4 rattles
- 2-3 teethers
- Playmat
- Books
- Doorway jumper
- Soft blocks
- Changing pad
- Changing pad cover
- Clothes hamper.

Bathtime

- Baby bathtub
- Baby soap
- Baby shampoo
- 2-4 soft towels or hooded baby towels
- Soft washcloths (keep apart from diaper washcloths)

Feeding

- 10-16 bottles and nipples, both 4- and 8- ounce
- Pump (if you plan to breastfeed)
- Milk storage bags (if you plan to breastfeed)
- Nursing pads (if you plan to breastfeed)
- Nipple cream (if you plan to breastfeed)
- Nursing pillow (if you plan to breastfeed)
- Bottle brush
- Dishwasher basket for small items
- 4-8 bibs
- Burp cloths
- 2-4 pacifiers
- Formula (if not nursing)

Health

- Baby nail clippers or blunt scissors
- Baby thermometer

- Petroleum jelly and sterile gauze (if you decide to circumcise)
- Infant first aid kit

Baby gear

- Infant or convertible car seat
- Stroller or infant carrier
- Baby swing or bouncer
- Playard with bassinet
- High chair

Keep in mind that each baby's needs are going to be unique, and use this list as a guide rather than a rule. If your baby is coming in the winter, you'll want to get warm clothing right away, but if they're coming in the summer, you can put off the coats and extra blankets for a bit.

There are also a few things that you might be tempted to put on your baby registry, but you can probably skip, such as:

Baby shoes – you can get socks and booties and skip the shoes until baby starts walking.

Crib bumpers – bumpers are a hazard and shouldn't be used.

Drop down crib – drop down cribs aren't manufactured anymore. If you are given a hand-me-down, check to make sure it abides by current safety standards.

Bottle warmer – bottle warmers can be convenient, but they really aren't necessary.

Dressy clothes – babies don't get out to many soirees, so if you don't have an upcoming event in your baby's first few months, just stick with the basics.

TOYS – If there's a specific toy you really want, go ahead and add it to your registry, but don't ask for a lot of toys as people will get you plenty anyway.

Diapers/newborn clothes – while these are important to have (we included them on our checklist), keep in mind that you'll likely get a lot of these items whether or not they're on your baby registry and use your best judgment when asking for them.

7

SETTING UP A NURSERY

"It takes a big heart to shape little minds".

— UNKNOWN

S etting up a nursery is part of the excitement of having a baby on the way. It can be fun and gratifying. However, for someone who has never designed a baby's room, it can be difficult to know where to start and what you actually need.

You can use this comprehensive guide to create a room that will be enjoyable and safe with every essential your child will need for the first year or two of life. Keep reading to learn everything you need to know!

DESIGNING A BABY NURSERY IN 4 STEPS

On the one hand, you may have a ton of ideas in your head on what you want to add to the baby's room. On the other hand, you may not. Use these recommendations to get your baby room design going.

PICK A THEME AND STYLE

An easy way to get started with designing the baby's room is picking a theme or style.You can find inspiration from children's books, cartoons, old baby prints, and novelty fabrics. You may like a Victorian style or prefer a more modern approach.

Take a bit of time to pick your theme and style because you don't want to find a better inspiration a few months down the road.

TIP: If you need inspiration then check out Pinterest. You can find millions of fresh ideas by just typing „nursery" to the search engine.

Selecting a theme and style helps narrow down many of the other choices you will need to make during the design process.

SHOP TEXTILES FIRST

Before you buy paint, you need to find the textiles you want to use in the room. The textiles can include wall hangings, bedding, curtain/shade fabrics, throw rugs, pillows, and furniture upholstery.

Remember, it's easier to find a paint chip that matches fabric than trying to match a particular material to a paint sample.

DECIDE ON YOUR COLOR SCHEME

With your theme in mind, style decided and textiles on hand; now it's time to select your color scheme. The wall color will likely be the most dominant color in the room, so choose it with care. Soothing pastels make the baby's room more restful. You can also draw on lighter colors and make the nursery really stand out.

Another consideration is how often you want to repaint the room. A good paint job can last five to ten years (barring toddler intervention with crayons, paint, and markers). Going with a neutral color will help you paint less often.

Go with one or two accent colors. A child's room often ends up being a jumble of color due to the proliferation of toys, books, and clothing. Limiting your accent colors will help them stand out amidst the chaos.

Which Colors to Pick?

It's said that rooms start to affect us in less than 10 seconds, so it's imperative to pick suitable colors for your nursery. All of them affect us in one way or another. Here you can see the basics of five popular colors.

When you decorate a room for an older child, take his or her temperament into account. For example, if your kid is very calm, you may want to decorate the room with little brighter energizing colors. Usually, it's the other way around though. Calming blue color is the top choice for many parents.

Shades of Blue: Blue is generally considered one of the most soothing colors and is good for intellectual work. It's a good idea to combine it with warmer tones though.

Shades of Green: Green promotes harmony and is good for concentration.

Pink: Pink is a soothing color, but using only pink makes the room feel draining.

White: White is a pure color, but use it too much, and the room may feel cold and unfriendly.

Orange and Yellow: These are two warm colors that are best combined with more soothing tones.

CONSIDER ALSO THE CEILING WHEN SETTING UP A NURSERY

In the first months of life, your infant will spend a lot of time on his or her back, looking up. Make the ceiling part of the decor. Paint the ceiling a soothing color and add a bit of interest with decals. Bring a mural up from the wall to the ceiling. Give the ceiling a starry sky.

Installing a ceiling fan is also a good idea for positive airflow and temperature control. A cold room makes it easier for the baby to sleep and helps to prevent SIDS.

You can find many ceiling fans specially designed for nurseries. However, if you don't want to change it out in a couple of years, a simple white one will do the trick.

FENG SHUI OF A BABY BED

You can treat feng shui as simple teaching on how to make rooms more suitable for us. Two-year-olds can already often tell where they want their beds to be. It's best to trust their instincts. But if you're still looking for a place for a baby crib, then a couple of pointers:

- Don't place the crib directly in front of a window

because, according to feng shui, the energy flow is too
intense for peaceful sleeping

- Place beds or cribs so that they face the door
- Placing many objects with sharp corners around a baby
  crib isn't advisable as they can cause scary shadows
- All cribs and most toddler beds already have high
  headboards, which make kids feel safe.

CREATE A PLACE TO NURSE

Whether you are breastfeeding or using formula, you will want
a place set up for feeding the baby.

Do you Need a Nursing Chair?

New parents usually buy a nursing chair (I'm no exception
here), but if you're tight on a budget or don't have much free
space, then I recommend waiting for a couple of weeks. It may
turn out that you don't miss it. For example, our boy preferred
lying next to his parents while eating and so the feeding usually
happened on a couch or our bed.

If you buy one, then get a comfortable, practical nursing chair
with a covering that is easy to clean. Arms on the chair will help
with positioning both you and the baby for a comfortable feeding, so it probably will make your life more comfortable. You
can also have a table with storage within easy reach of the chair
so you can have everything you need on hand.

Nursing chairs may be stationary or ones that glide. You can't lock a traditional rocking chair into place to prevent finger pinching as the child grows older so a glider may be a better option if you wish to buy a moving chair.

Make Your Window Coverings Functional and Beautiful

Long, long time ago in 1999 Nature published a study. It suggested that the absence of a nightly period of full darkness in early childhood may be a risk factor in the development of nearsightedness (myopia). Subsequent studies since show that it probably isn't true. So you can safely continue using your night light. That said, if you live in a city like me, then the incoming light is quite bright, and it can cause sleep problems by reducing the amount of melatonin. Melatonin is a substance in your body that regulates your sleep rhythm.

So there's at least one good reason to install blackout curtains or shades to darken the room for the night. As a bonus, some shades reflect heat so you can keep the room cooler for your baby.

As I've noted before, it's a good idea to buy the window coverings before painting, but install them after the job's done. It's so much easier to paint an empty room.

BABY NURSERY LIGHTING

Give the Room Multiple Lighting Options When Setting up a Nursery

Your baby's room should have multiple lighting options. As I've explained before (sorry for repeating myself), exposing your little to bright light before sleeping may cause sleeping problems.

If the room has an overhead lighting fixture, you can install a dimmer switch on it. This will allow you to adjust the light as needed.

Nighttime feedings are more comfortable if you have a second lamp next to the nursing chair. Many lamps have a dimmer switch, so you are able to adjust the light level on the second lamp. This lamp can also serve as a lamp for story time. If you have a floor lamp, then it's a good idea to remove it after your baby starts to crawl because they are easily knocked over.

Nigh Lights

Nightlights are safe to use and can comfort your older kid if he or she is afraid of the dark. At the floor level, they can be useful for safety reasons- you can see enough to avoid tripping on anything.

I haven't yet bought one for my nursery because I want that my all my kids to get used to sleeping in the dark. Thanks to the baby monitor, I don't have a need to go into the nursery while he's sleeping.

SANITATION - BUT DON'T OVERDO IT

Fear of germs or germophobia seems to be a big issue among new parents but try to get over it. Our bodies carry approximately as many bacteria as we have human cells and what's important is the balance. If your baby is exposed to too few bacteria, it may actually be harmful to his or her. For example, the risk of allergies and some chronic diseases rises.

Keep the nursery clean, but use pure water. You rarely need harsh chemicals to clean the room.

Suggestions:

- Select your furniture with easy cleaning in mind
- All textiles should be washable
- Create a place to store cleaning supplies so you can clean up messes without leaving the room
- Know where you are going to dispose of diapers and store soiled clothing.

II

NOW A DAD – GUIDE TO BONDING BEST

Yahoo! You have been waiting 9 months for this, and here it is! Your new baby is finally here! Now what do you do? You can scarcely imagine that you have brought this new life into the world. You want the best for your newborn! You will be responsible for influencing this new soul that you have produced. That's a tremendous responsibility! Everything begins with the bonding that you create with your baby.

WHY DOES IT MATTER ANYWAY?

A growing body of research has shown that when dads spend time with their newborns and begin developing a strong relationship with them from the very beginning, they reap a number of benefits.

A child's physical and mental development is significantly boosted when his dad has played with him from the start, compared to children whose fathers took a more hands-off approach.

Fathers experience less stress and increased confidence when they have their own special time with their newborns.

Strong father-child bonds can help counter issues such as depression later on in life.

Men who report that they had a good relationship with their fathers during childhood were found to be better equipped to handle stress.

Children who experienced close interactions with their fathers from an early age tend to be more successful academically, have better relationships with their peers and be less likely to get involved with crime or abuse drugs and alcohol.

8

PLAYMATE - GROWING A BOND

"When she wakes up in the morning, she gets all excited when she sees or hears me. You can't buy that type of feeling."

— VETERAN DAD

O f all the powerful roles in humanity, a father teaching his baby to play has got to be the coolest. Playing, your baby's main job teaches him how to laugh and take risks. It develops his motor skills and speeds the development of his brain and nervous system. Very serious stuff.

As a father, you're designed to be his perfect playmate. Flight lessons, peek-a-boo, and wrestling all come naturally. Furthermore, playing is bonding at its finest. Dads elicit the most radiant smiles and infectious belly laughs, sometimes with just a wink.

There's a time I saw a first-time father seeking advice on Reddit; saying he had a daughter who had just turned 3 months old. So, he took 2 months off work to spend time with her and the wife after a little rough birth experience that led the baby to NICU and put his wife in ICU.

Fast forward, he said "I've read all the books, give baths, bottle feed(my wife did breastfeed for a while), try and play games(she is not very active yet, at least with her hands), change diapers. I do everything I possibly can to be involved and helpful..."

"But at the end of it, my baby seems very indifferent towards me, doesn't smile too much at me, but lights up with her mom, when she wakes up from a nap and I go and comfort her, she starts screaming but if her mom comes up... she sorta sighs and calms down WITH JUST SEEING her... and the worst part is when I do try and put her to sleep she most likely will fuss unless I am feeding her and she falls asleep at the bottle... she doesn't look at me when I am holding her a majority of the time, but she stares at my wife whenever she is holding her and my wife doesn't have to do much to get her to fall asleep in her arms..."

"I on the other hand have to jump through hoops and fussing to put her to sleep... My wife is a great mom, but I just feel like so much effort is wasted... simply because my wife's best friends also had a baby and her husband doesn't do anything with the child, and the baby obviously fusses when he is with him... so if the results are the same, I sometimes feel I shouldn't try as hard..." "I just wish my daughter would look at me for comfort like she does my wife." - He said.

My suggestion could've been "play harder, new daddy!" Sometimes, the bond is instant; parents fall in love the moment they set eyes on their little "bundle of joy." Other times, bonding with the baby takes longer. The same can be said for the babies; they may (or may not) feel connected to you immediately.

In fact, studies have found that about 20% of new parents feel no real emotional attachment to their newborn in the hours after delivery. Sometimes, it takes weeks or even months to feel that attachment. If you haven't begun bonding with your baby (or vice versa), don't feel anxious or guilty - it should come with time.

Think about it this way; have you ever had a cold that lasts an entire month? Your condition becomes the norm. "Healthy" no longer seems possible. Well, then it's just the same damn scenario.

The important thing to realize is that it doesn't make you a bad parent and, thankfully, there are several things you can do to encourage and improve your burgeoning relationship with your baby.

GUIDELINES FOR PLAYING

While playing with babies comes naturally to dads, there are a few things to keep in mind:

Short Field of Vision at First

For the first couple of weeks, a baby's vision is fuzzy and he'll fixate on things that are about a foot from his eyes. Place a picture or toy with highly contrasting colors in his line of sight to catch his attention, and then move it back and forth slowly so he can track it.

Her Favorite Mug - Yours

She'll focus on your face and recognizes it in about one month. While she likes mom's face too, your whiskers make yours more interesting. For some reason, at around six months, babies like to grab dad's nose and try to pull it off.

Stop When She's Had Enough

She may be finished before you are, and it's important to recognize the signs before you irritate her. If she turns her face away, arches her back, or whimpers when you expect her to be having fun, assume she's worn out or overstimulated and it's time to quit.

Be Careful He Doesn't Get Scared

Getting scared will not just trigger crying; remember all those neurons firing for the first time? You want your baby wired to trust you and his new environment and not grow up anxious. Be gentle and careful about situations—sudden loud noises, people getting too close or picking him up roughly—that may frighten him.

Nurture an Adventurous Spirit

Notice when he's reaching out for something and encourage his exploration. Let him take his time. Let him try for something just beyond his reach. Before you do something for him, let him try to do it himself. Encourage, don't frustrate.

Improvise

Put your creative stamp on playing with your baby; build your repertoire of games that only he (and you) know. Opportunities abound; make your sock into a puppet that sings to him. Dip his toe in ice cream and give him a taste. Blow raspberries on his tummy, stopping and starting a couple of times until he's bouncing with anticipation, then cut loose with a big one.

Just You and Him – Anything Goes

There's no one else around? It's time for ELVIS! Or whatever you like. Got a comedy act buried deep? Drag it out. No matter how bad you truly are, she'll think you're the best.

IT'S A DIRTY JOB AND IT'S DAD'S - GAMES TO PLAY

Here are things to do with your baby from birth through six months. Try them, see what works, and then come up with your own. Getting in even five minutes of play each day is a good start.

0 TO 2 MONTHS

There's always something you can do to engage your baby. Here are some ideas to get you going:

Monkey See, Monkey Do

She might mimic you sticking your tongue out, even as a newborn. As she grows, she may mimic your other facial expressions and cooing sounds, too. Start early: hold her face-to-face, smile, open your mouth and slowly stick out your tongue. Repeat.

Airplane

Hold your baby firmly with both hands—one under her bottom and the other cupped on the back of her head. Lift her in the air and let her "fly" around slowly and gently. Always firmly support her head.

Pull-Ups

Put his face up in your lap, and place one finger in each of his hands so he grabs on. Then pull him up a little, let him down, and repeat.

Baby Calisthenics

With your baby on her back, gently pull her legs up to you and then side to side. Up, out, down, back, reverse. Do the same with her arms.

Walking at One Month

Their walking reflex is very cool. Using both hands to hold him, stand him on the bed and lean him forward. He'll slowly raise one foot as if taking a step and if you move him forward, he'll take another.

Record Your Babbler

When he starts cooing and babbling away, grab your phone, load a voice recorder app, and hit "record." Then play it back to him and watch the fascination in his eyes and the smile on his face. Do the same with his fussing, and he'll stop to take in this new distraction. Keep the recording; it'll be a special memory.

2 TO 4 MONTHS

Your baby will become more active at two to four months, smiling and starting to coo and babble away, and responding more during playtime. She'll love having fun with you, especially when you smile and talk to her. The possibility for games increases; examples include:

Mattress Trampoline

Lay your baby on her back on the bed. Push down on the mattress so that she bounces a little bit. Go slowly and gently so she enjoys it and doesn't get anxious or upset. Remember, she's still learning to trust you, so don't ramp up the action to a level your child isn't yet comfortable with.

Kick Boxing

With your baby lying on his back, put the palms of your hands up so they are nearly touching the soles of his feet. Gently push his foot with your hand, switching back and forth between right and left. Soon, you'll do nothing but hold your hands there and your baby will kick them in the same right to left pattern you initiate.

Baby Acrobatics

Sit on the ground with your baby facing you in your lap. Get a firm grip around his midsection and rollback, holding him up in the air while you say "wheee!" If he loves it—and, there's a good chance he will—you'll be priming him for past-times that will terrify you later in life.

Lots of Belly Time

Since we put our babies to sleep on their backs, they have few opportunities to develop upper body strength by lifting their heads and pushing themselves up with their hands. So give him plenty of belly time while playing, and he'll be the fastest crawler in his Mommy & Me group.

4 TO 6 MONTHS

Your baby is quickly becoming bigger, stronger, more active, and responsive. This opens up a whole new range of possibilities. Babies love to be cheered on at this age, so don't hold back.

Peek-a-Boo

Always a favorite. Put your hands in front of your face for a few moments, then jerk them away and say "peek-a-boo!" Repeat about five times, then put her hands over her eyes and show her how to do it. Over time, she'll catch on and after a month or so you'll be peek-a-booing back and forth with her giggling away.

Her First Song

When she's cooing or babbling, take her hand and place the back of it over her mouth to cork her briefly, then lift it and repeat. The result will be bah-bah-bah, which she'll find fascinating as well as a new trick to enthrall her adoring audience (Mom, Grandma).

Rock 'n' Roll

He'll love this one, though mom may not. Raid the kitchen for wooden spoons and a few pots and use them to make some serious music. Put a spoon in his chubby little hand and show him how to bang a pot like a drum, then cut him loose to bang away on his own. As he flails away, make sure he doesn't inadvertently bang his head or yours.

Hide and Seek

Take something your baby is playing with and hide it inside or underneath something bigger. If it's a cloth book, put it underneath a light blanket. If it's a block, put it inside a plastic bowl. Show him where it is and then hide it again until he finds it himself.

Crawler In Training

Put him on his belly, sideways over a towel. Grab both towel ends in one hand and lift him up a few inches, supporting him with your other hand. Get him on his hands and knees, and start moving his arms and legs one at a time in a crawling motion. While this maneuver may not actually teach him to crawl, he'll find it interesting and maybe even fun—it can't hurt.

LEVEL YOUR GAME UP

Skin to Skin Contact

It is one of the most gorgeous ways to bond with your baby… and it's not just for mums!

When you hold your baby next to your warm skin, baby can hear your heartbeat, snuggle into your chest (whether hairy or not for dads!), and smell your scent.

Babies prefer the real smell of you, so don't go too heavy on the deodorant on perfumes. Skin-to-skin contact can be done anytime; watching the TV, reading, listen to music, dancing to music.

Every time you hold a baby like this we are drawn to look at them and them to look up into our faces. This promotes lifelong bonding and encourages the release of huge amounts of the love hormone, oxytocin.

The other thing skin-to-skin contact does is reduces stress hormone and helps babies to drift off into la-la land and sleep well. Now if that isn't a good excuse to promote it, I don't know what is.

Get Out And About

It's important to try and get out of the house, to the park, the shops, or the library.

The outside world is great for giving you things to talk about with your baby, whether it's the ducks in the park, the cars in the street, or the fruit and veg at the supermarket.

Try and stop to get face-to-face with your baby as you stroll. This will let you see what's grabbing their attention more easily, and you can talk about that.

On your travels, keep an eye out for things that are happening in your community. There might be a group out there that's calling for you and your skills.

For example, in Blackpool, there is a community shed for dads to come along and create things for their kids.

So if you've spent years tinkering with bikes, cars, or computers, that practice making things could come in handy! Find as many ways to speak to your baby as you can. It's important to start talking to babies as early as you can.

This gets babies used to hearing your voice and responding, even before they can form words. And think about it, before baby can complain, it's the ideal time to practice your "dad jokes"!

It's great to be daft with your baby. If you're smiling and happy, chances are you'll get a smile out of them, even if the jokes themselves don't get them chuckling (yet...).

It's always good to try and speak to babies face-to-face and to look for signs that they're trying to communicate.

Encourage them to babble (that's when they make noises like they're doing baby speak) by leaving them time to respond after you speak to them. Think of it like tennis, waiting for a return every time you talk.

Become Number One Storyteller

Storytelling is a role that dads can really revel in. Try having a bit of 'story time' each day when you're with your baby. Not only will it help in creating a strong bond with you, but also a great way to help your child learn language.

You can tell stories you know, or make up stories on the spot. Be as daft as you want, make up whatever characters you like.

Or, you could read stories out from a book. But you don't need to read books word for word. In fact, it's better if you can point out pictures, put on voices and make noises.

In Blackpool, dads are taking part in woodwork classes, creating figures based on the stories they tell to their children. That way they have toys that bring their stories to life. So, if you're handy with making things, why not have a go at making some characters yourself? You don't have to use wood, just make sure it's a safe material, and don't let your baby try to eat the figures!

Make Connections With Other Dads

Chances are, a lot of new dads and soon-to-be dads have similar hopes and fears to you.

By meeting other dads, you'll be able to share your experiences and help each other out. Once you're both laughing at the things that worry you, they're bound to lose their edge.

A good way to meet other dads is to try and make it out to classes and groups with your partner.

You might feel a bit uncomfortable striking up conversations with the other guys in waiting rooms, but every man you see in these places is in a similar boat. They might need a 'dad buddy' to help them make sense of it all too.

If you are struggling and you're not sure who to speak with, then there are places online that offer help too.

9

FEEDING YOUR TOT

"The way to a man's heart is through his stomach"

— IAN SOMERHALDER

The old days of Mom being the caregiver and Dad's interaction with Baby limited to "Wave to Daddy, honey" is over. Today, lots of dads are involved in baby care and child-rearing in ways that would make our grandfathers shudder. More and more fathers are doing more and more to share parenting with mothers. Even breastfeeding moms are making it possible for dads to bottle feed baby—may be out of necessity, maybe to encourage a father-child bond, maybe to improve their bond with Dad.

Yet there are still few resources available to help new dads learn what to do for and with their infant. Here, I share wih you a simple guide:

FINDING THE DAMN BOTTLE

Buying the right bottle is the same as shopping for any of the million other things you need but would prefer not to have to shell out for. Start with the cheaper bottles from Coles or Woolworths and then get progressively more expensive as your baby decides that you being a tight-arse is not in their best interests.

Bottles from the supermarkets can cost as little as $10. This is a great thing if your baby takes to them. Otherwise, like me, you could find yourself shelling out upwards of $50 for fancy-pants soft silicone bottles which are meant to mimic the feel of the breast (this is not as exciting as it sounds).

Fabulous for baby but not ideal for you. You will lose them and have a minor heart attack every time you have to pay for another.

PREPARING THE BOTTLE

Breastmilk Preparation:

Frozen breastmilk can be thawed overnight in the fridge, or by placing the bag under warm running water. Gradual warming is key, so if you want to thaw breast milk faster, use something like the Dr. Brown's MilkSpa that safely warms breast milk without removing important nutrients. Before putting the milk in the bottle, make sure it's clean by giving it a quick wash (as well as your hands).

Formula Preparation:

Whether you will be using formula exclusively or supplementing, there are a few tricks to making the most out of each bottle.

Wash the bottle, parts, and your hands before mixing. Follow the formula maker instructions for mixing guidelines but make sure to measure precisely, as too much powder can cause an upset stomach for your little one. Mix thoroughly, ensuring there are no clumps that can get stuck in the nipple. Remember that formula stays good for two hours at room temp or 24 hours if refrigerated.

GETTING THE TEMP RIGHT

No baby likes cold milk. Even in summer, room temperature is better than cold. Fussy little …

Anyway, you have options. Automatic drivers will prefer the bottle warmer. Milk in the bottle, bottle in warmer, press the button and wait for the beep – unless you don't want to spend the $80+ it will cost for a half-decent warmer. Or if like my son's, your bottle is silicone, it'll warm up as quickly as a 1978 BMW 3 Series. Fun times.

Your other option is to plonk the bottle in a bowl of warm water. This takes a while to heat but it's predictable and works on all types of bottles. And it's free.

Don't forget to swirl the milk to get rid of hot spots. If the milk is too hot, but will still try to drink it but will likely come off after every sip. Don't force it. Fridge for a few minutes, or a splash of cold pre-boiled water, will do the job.

PUTTING ON THE SHOW

Relax And Be Confident

Baby won't know nervousness when she feels it, but she will sense that something is not right. If you aren't relaxed, neither will she be. If she isn't relaxed she won't eat well, or if she does eat, it won't stay down. If you are nervous, take some deep breaths, stretch your back, shake out your hands, and look at that little bundle—she is depending on you. You got this!

Act as if it is: even if you aren't feeling 100% confident in your bottle-feeding skills, act as if you were. Eventually, the act becomes the reality.

Get Comfortable

Feeding a baby is not something that can be rushed. You can't do it while you are on the go or in a quick minute between other tasks. Kick-off your shoes and find a comfortable seat; you'll be there for about half an hour. The more comfortable you and Baby are, the better he will eat. Make feeding time a ritual and you and your baby will enjoy it better.

Bottle feeding baby might just give you an excuse to hang on to that recliner your mother-in-law has been complaining about.

Find The Right Position

The milk or formula flows much faster from the bottle than it does from the breast. To keep Baby from choking or having to gulp, hold her in a more upright position than breastfeeding mom does—more of a 45-degree incline, rather than 90 degrees sitting up or lying flat on her back. It can be difficult to find the right position, but you'll keep trying because you want the best for Baby.

It will take some practice to find what's most comfortable for you, and what works best for your baby.

Feeling The Flow

Flow is a tricky thing. Different teats have different flows and while you will obviously start with the lowest flow when your baby is a newborn, knowing when to move up to a faster one is tricky and messy. Sorry, but it's just trial and error here.

It is likely that bub will look like a rubbish contestant in an eating competition for a while. It all goes roughly towards the mouth, some of it in, some of it out, and then some that went in comes out again. Don't wear your crisp white business shirt from Mr. Lauren while you do this! Milk is nowhere near as white as you think it is.

Here's a trick anyway - Wait for the latch

Whether you start bottle feeding after the baby has got the hang of nursing with mom, or immediately after he's born, be sure to make sure that your baby's lips are sealed around the nipple of the bottle. Your baby has limited to no experience sucking. First, check if the nipple of the bottle is on the tongue, not under it. You'll have to help by to gently pushing his lower lip up to the nipple.

Have patience as both of you are learning a new skill.

Look At Your Baby

According to some studies, babies can recognize faces after only a few days. Be sure to look at and engage with your baby as you feed him. You can sing or talk to him, too. These are the first days, weeks, and months of a lifetime relationship. The more you and Baby get to know one another, the more comfortable both of you will be. This is the start of you being his go-to guy.

Be aware, though, intense eye contact may distract your baby from the act of nursing.

Take Off Your Shirt Papa

Skin-to-skin contact has amazing health benefits for your baby, so strip off that shirt. After spending months near mom's heart, babies benefit from skin-to-skin contact in several ways. Their breathing and heart rate stabilize by being near yours; their body begins to learn to regulate their internal temperature, and they are generally happier. If the air is cool, cover both of you with a blanket. As a plus, not wearing a shirt will eliminate stains on that shirt.

Some babies prefer to be swaddled, that is, wrapped tightly in their blankies. Even when swaddling, you can accomplish skin-to-skin contact with your child's head.

Switch Arms

Burping time is a good time to switch arms. When you are feeding Baby, you'll be holding him with one arm and holding the bottle with the other. Switching baby from one arm to the other mimics the breastfeeding mom and provides both you and baby some relief from staying in the same position. Changing arms eases pressure on your back and Baby's neck and back. It also gives Baby a new perspective on the world and allows you to enjoy another view of that precious face.

You may find that you are more comfortable holding a baby on one side. Try to learn to be comfortable on both sides, as the baby should switch from time to time.

Finally: Fall in Love

Probably the most important tip for feeding your baby is to just do it. Bottle feeding your child provides a definite huge benefit, one that you won't get from changing diapers and taking out the trash.

The best part about bottle feeding your baby is that you have to opportunity for uninterrupted one-on-one time with your new love. Take this time to fall deeply in love with that little person. Touch those little toes, feel him breathe along with you, kiss his little forehead. Love him like you'll never love another.

Bottle feeding—more than any other action Dad can take in the first year—creates a bond between Daddy and Baby. Dads who take an active role in the early years of their kids' lives are more involved in the later years. There's no better way to get involved than by bottle feeding. You are creating a lifelong bond.

You'll need this bond when he becomes a teenager.

BURPING IT UP!

Do you know how good it feels to burp sometimes? Sometimes babies need the same kind of relief. And helping them burp can be a good Dad job.

But first. Burping is a little over-rated. People sometimes act like parents have to make sure their babies burp at absolutely every feeding.

Not really.

In cultures where babies are carried upright all the time, in slings or on their mother's back, parents "burping their babies" is unheard of. Babies who are carried a lot often just burp when they need to on their own. So, carry your baby around against your shoulder after a feeding and see what happens.

If she's fallen asleep don't feel you have to wake her up to burp her. Leave her be.

On the other hand, there are situations where burping might not be a bad idea:

If the baby had been crying for a while before feeding, she may have swallowed air while crying and need help in bringing it up.

If you are feeding your baby with a bottle, she might swallow air if her lips didn't make a good seal around the bottle nipple.

If you or your partner think the baby needs burping. A lot of early parenting is guesswork. You try things and see if it helps. If you think your baby might be swallowing air, or might need to burp, go for it. Believe us, there are no support groups for adults who were burped too often as babies.

Here are three different ways to burp... the baby.

The Classic.

Try putting him high up on your shoulder so that your shoulder presses just below his tiny ribcage, then gently pat his back. Oh, and, um, put receiving blanket or burp pad on your shoulder first. Trust us on this one!

Sit-down burping.

Drape the baby across your lap, which puts a little pressure on his tummy, and pat his back gently. You might have to experiment a bit to find a position that feels right.

The "folding" technique sometimes works with small babies. Hold him in a sitting position, with one hand supporting his chin (so his head doesn't flop forward) then gently bend him forward a little bit, chest toward knees. Then straighten him up again. Repeat a couple more times.

No need to push it. If you don't hear a satisfying belch after a minute or two, chances are there's no burp to come up. However, if your baby starts to grimace or wiggle around as though he's uncomfortable when you lay him down, it's worth giving it another try.

Spitting up.

Lots of babies spit up small amounts of swallowed milk after some feedings. Some do it after just about every feeding. It's normal and although people have looked for ways to prevent it, there is no proven solution. If your baby is a spitter-upper - you'll know - just always keep a receiving blanket over your shoulder if you're holding the baby right after feeding. Oh and buy laundry detergent when it's on sale. You'll need extra.

10

BATHING AND DRESSING A NEWBORN

"Baby, baby, baby oooh. Like baby, baby, baby nooo"

— JUSTIN BIEBER

W hen it comes to newborn bath time, the more hands, the better — in other words, make the first few baths a team effort. Set up beforehand, and do it when you're feeling calm. (Breathe. In…out…in. Good.) Commit to letting voicemail pick up any calls — for this project, all your attention should be on baby.

Here's what you need for a successful bath time:

Washing station

Whether you bathe baby in a sink lined with a soft surface or a plastic tub with a sling placed in the real bath, your setup should be steady and there shouldn't be anything hard or sharp for baby to accidentally knock against. Position baby's head away from the faucet (and use a soft faucet cover, if you have one).

Warm room

Keep the temperature raised so it's not a shock to baby's system when she comes out of the bath. Babies have a hard time regulating their core temperature, so they shouldn't be chilled for too long.

Water

Fill the tub about three inches with water a little bit warmer than lukewarm. Submerge your entire hand and wrist to check the temperature. The water shouldn't be running while baby is in the tub, because the depth could quickly become dangerous, or the water temperature could change and become too hot. (Tip: Turn your water heater down to 120 degrees to avoid accidental scalding.)

Plastic pitcher or cup

Use this to pour water over baby and rinse her off. (This is safer and less scary for babies than the gush of water coming from a faucet.) Or squeeze a washcloth soaked in water over baby's head to rinse.

Soap

Though some moms prefer to use only water on their newborns, the sweat and dead skin that accumulate on baby can produce an odor that makes soap pretty welcome. Go easy on the amount, though, because too much can dry out baby's skin. Look for a mild, tear-free cleanser that can be used for both baby's body and hair. (Even tear-free soap should be kept away from baby's eyes and face, though.) Some parents prefer all-natural baby wash, so that's good too. Bottles that open with one hand or use a lockable pumping mechanism are best, because they allow you to keep that one necessary hand on baby at all times. If baby has a hard time with the washcloth, just put soap on your hands and clean him that way.

Washcloths

Designate a certain color or pattern used specifically for bath time — you wouldn't want to confuse them with your diaper cloths!

Any special treatments

Diaper cream, cradle cap treatment, or any other remedies your doctor has recommended should be within reach.

Timing

Pay attention to baby's mood after bath time, and use it to your advantage. If he's energetic and ready to play, bathe during the day. If he seems more mellow, make it a pre-bedtime activity.

STEP BY STEP PROCEDURE:

Start by soaking baby a little. Always keep one hand on baby, and remember that infants are especially slippery when wet. If baby needs cradle cap treatment, put this on first, then come back to rinse after you've washed the rest of his body.

Otherwise, start from the top and work your way down. Wash the face first, cleaning one area at a time — it can be scary for infants to have their entire face covered with a washcloth. As you move down the body, thoroughly wash inside all the folds (including under the arms, in the neck and the genital area).

Sweat and skin can get stuck in those areas and fester, causing nasty rashes, so it's important to keep them as clean and dry as possible. Save baby's dirtiest parts (aka the diaper area) for last. Then, move back up and wash baby's hair.

Since infants lose most of their heat through their heads, this should be your very last move. If the water is still warm you can engage in a little playtime, but resist the urge to splash for too long — as the water chills, baby will quickly get cold.

There's no need to bathe more than every few days. Since babies' skin is so dry it can dehydrate quickly, so it's actually best not to wash daily. Some parents even get by with as little as once a week. As one doctor put it, "When they start to smell funny, you know it's time for a bath."

BATH-SIDE SETUP:

Towels

Keep a few towels on hand — one to carefully dry out all the little folds, and then another one fresh out of the dryer (but not too hot) to wrap baby up in. (Roll it up to keep in the warmth.) Hooded towels are also a good buy.

- Clean diaper
- Clean clothes
- Blanket
- Lotion

Some babies love lotion massages after bath time. Remember, though — flaking skin isn't necessarily dry. Babies accumulate dead skin that needs to come off.

- Hairbrush or comb
- For those babies blessed with tresses.

Note: Until the cord stump falls off (about 7 to 9 days) and the circumcision is healed, baby should only have sponge baths. Wrap baby in a towel to keep him warm, then pull out one limb at a time to wash with a sponge and warm water. The cord stump can get infected, so it should always be kept clean and dry. If it seems dirty or sticky, wash it with soap and water and then dry well using a clean cloth.

DRESS AND UNDRESS A BABY

Dressing and undressing your baby is wonderful face-to-face time that you can spend interacting with each other. Talking to your baby calmly can help keep her relaxed during the process. When putting clothes on or taking clothes off your baby, always make sure to:

Handle your baby carefully and gently. Work slowly and tell him what you're doing. As you dress and undress your baby more often, you'll become more comfortable and the process will go more smoothly.

Remove clothes with care. When removing any item of clothing, work to carefully loosen it. Be careful to not twist your baby or move too quickly to avoid overextending his arms or legs or putting him into any uncomfortable positions.

Choose the correct size clothes. You don't want to dress your baby in clothes that are too short or too tight. The neck of any shirt should be comfortable and the legs should be long enough so that he can extend his legs.

Make sure your baby's clothes are safe. If your baby's clothes have buttons or decorations, make sure they are securely stitched so that she cannot remove them.

Choose layers when dressing your little one. Dressing newborns in layers is a great way to make sure that they are warm and comfortable. Layers can be easily added or removed depending on the temperature and your baby's comfort level. A good rule of thumb: Dress your baby in as many layers as you are wearing, with perhaps one more on hand to add on in case your baby gets cold.

Place your baby on a safe, flat surface. Lay a blanket down to cushion the surface.

HOW TO DRESS A BABY

When putting a shirt over your baby's head, gather the entire shirt like an accordion up to the neck. Holding the opening of the neck, carefully place the shirt over your baby's head and slowly pull the shirt over her body.

Gather the sleeves up to the cuff and put your baby's hand through the opening. Carefully work the sleeve up the rest of her arm.

When putting on pants, start at your baby's feet and gradually work the outfit up her body.

If you need to fasten the back of an outfit, gently turn your baby on to her tummy or sit her up with support.

HOW TO UNDRESS A BABY

Begin at your baby's head and carefully loosen and slide the outfit down over the body.

Be sure to support your baby's head and body with one hand as you lift him to reposition clothes. Remember to avoid twisting or jerking any of your baby's limbs at any time.

Carefully unsnap each snap and loosen or rearrange the item until it can be easily removed. For instance, use two hands to remove the socks gently rather than pulling them off the feet.

If you need to turn your baby on his side, be sure to support his body weight.

To get a bodysuit or shirt off of your little one, carefully lift her up off the table, and support her head and body. Slowly remove sleeves, working down toward the wrist.

11

BECOMING A DIAPER-CHANGING MACHINE

> *"Politicians and diapers must be changed often, and for the same reason."*
>
> — MARK TWAIN

D iaper changing is not for the faint of heart. I say this because I've seen grown men gag and throw up at the sight of baby poop. Some cringe with just the smell of the baby excrements. Well, this chapter is a call to you, first-time dad, to suck it up and face the truth. Your baby will poop, and diapers need to be changed.

You can rely on your partner or the nanny, but the skill comes in handy when you're alone with your little one. Moreover, by doing this task, you lighten the load for mom. So give your lady a break and take on this challenge.

This is bonding time with your baby. Of course, the poop can be a turn-off but spending quality time knows no limitations. The first few tries will still make you squeamish. However, as you change more nappies, the easier it becomes.

Furthermore, you will find your own technique and the best way to master your new art. I've done it and I'm sure all dads out there can do it as well. It's one activity every dad should experience. When you experience changing your baby's nappies, you'll never look at baby poop the same way again.

Before practically changing those nappies, however, there are a few things that your new daddy brain needs to know.

DIFFERENT KINDS OF BABY POOP

Let's first talk about the different kinds of poop. I bring this up because in the hospital it seems like the doctors and nurses are very interested/concerned in how many times your newborn has pooped and peed. They are interested and/or concerned for good reason since all this indicates if everything is working internally.

Poop from newborns for the first few days will look like a combination of motor oil and caramel. It is very sticky. This kind of poop is called meconium. It looks this way because it is made up of the stuff (intestinal epithelial cells, lanugo, mucus, amniotic fluid, bile, and water) your baby ingested while in utero. You will find that meconium is hard to clean off your baby's bum, but the good news is that it does not smell bad.

The second kind of poop you will see from your newborn will be what is called transitional poop. This poop happens usually between 2 and 4 days old. It's lighter in color than meconium (kind of army green and less sticky). Transitional poop is a sign that your newborn is beginning to digest early breast milk or formula and that everything is okay with his intestinal tract. This poop will last for the first week of life.

After transitional poop comes breastfed poop. This kind of poop often looks like Dijon mustard (yellow and/or greenish) with cottage cheese mixed in. It also may be dotted with seedlike flecks. For the benefit of fathers who struggle with poopy diapers this kind of poop does not smell all that bad.

If your baby is not breastfed then he will be formula fed which means his poop will look different. Formula-fed or bottle-fed poop is brown with a thick and creamy consistency. If the formula you give your newborn is iron-fortified then his poop will be dark brown or dark green.

When baby poop starts to get smelly is when you start feeding your baby solid foods like infant cereal, pureed bananas, and stuff like that. This kind of poop is called solid-food poop. It's brown or dark brown and thicker than peanut butter, but still mushy.

LET'S TAKE THE STINK OUT!

Step 1: Have everything you need within reach.

I usually open up the new diaper ready for use. My wife has a changing bag with everything needed in it. This beats having to fumble with stuff every time we need to change our baby's diaper. This also ensures that everything we need is available.

Here are the things that you need: changing pad, new diaper, plastic bag for the soiled diaper, cotton or gauze pad for wiping the baby, baby wipes (don't use wipes with alcohol, they can irritate your baby's skin), anti-rash cream, petroleum jelly.

Step 2: Wash your hands and sanitize.

You should also remove your ring, bracelets, or any accessories that may scrape your child's skin. It is also a good idea to warm your hands first before you touch your baby. Cold hands can be uncomfortable for them.

Step 3: Place your baby on the changing table or bed.

Note: Changing tables have straps to secure your baby so use them. For those who do have changing tables, your bed or any flat surface is good enough. Just make sure you put a blanket or towel underneath your baby to make it comfortable. Likewise, ensure that there is ample space for the baby.

Step 4: Unstrap & Fold.

Unstrap the dirty diaper and fold the flaps so it does not stick to your baby's skin. Some diapers don't use sticky tape but it is still a good idea to fold it back.

Step 5: Fold-down the top part of the dirty diaper.

This will expose the baby to poop. Some poop may still be sticking to your baby's skin so scoop them off with the top part of the used diaper or you can use a damp cotton/cloth to do this. If the skin is sensitive, you can use sterile gauze. Make sure you clean the whole area.

Note: To avoid infections, use a top to bottom motion when cleaning the genital area - especially when the baby is a girl. Also, change cotton or gauze frequently.

Step 6: Remove the soiled diaper underneath the baby and replace it with a new one.

Some suggest placing the new diaper underneath the baby even before you unfasten and clean the baby. But it does not work for me. You can try it if you want.

Note: place the soiled diaper away from your baby's reach. I've had numerous incidences I don't wish to share. Suffice to say, they were not pretty.

Step 7 Before securing the new diaper, make sure your baby is dry.

Also, this is the time to put on anti-rash cream, ointments or petroleum jelly, or whatever your doctor recommends. Once done, fasten the straps of the new diaper.

Note: Make sure that the diaper is not too tight or too loose. Also, the right size of diaper should always be used. Lastly, the weight recommendation on the diaper's label is just a guide. There are times when you need to experiment on the best size for your baby.

Step 8 Sanitize your hands before picking up your baby.

You must keep your hands and surroundings clean.

Congratulations, you just changed your baby's diaper. Now, get ready to do this 6 to 8 times a day. Don't worry, as your child grows, the need to change diapers becomes less frequent.

PRO TIPS TO DIAPERS

Pick the right diapers

Choosing the right diaper can be daunting, especially because the market is filled with numerous options with varied features. However, knowing your baby's needs will help you pick the right one.

Opt for a super-absorbent diaper, so it can absorb multiple wettings and ensures maximum protection from built-up damp-ness, and prevents rashes.

Make sure you select the right size diaper for a baby as the wrong size will either be too tight, which may cause marks on the baby's skin, or too loose, which may allow waste to escape.

Select a soft and breathable diaper material that is soothing for the baby's skin and prevents irritation and rashes.

Using ultra-thin or lightweight diapers

These days, Ultra products are also available, where the real innovation is to keep the diaper super lightweight, yet their absorption is more than double of regular diapers. This helps as they are lightweight and breathable and also let your baby stay active and comfortable. Remember, a heavyweight diaper doesn't just cause skin rashes but can also make a baby's movements a little slow because of the weight. So, switch to ultra-products for active comfort throughout.

Disposing diapers correctly

Dirty diapers should be properly cleaned and disposed of in the right manner to maintain a healthy and hygienic surrounding environment. If possible, shake the diaper content into the toilet before disposing of it. Then roll up the diaper as tightly as possible into a ball and reseal the adhesive tapes to hold it in place. You can also wrap the diaper in old newspapers and then dispose of it to avoid any odor or spillage. Ensure you wash your hands after you dispose of them.

Cleaning Boys vs Girls

The crucial difference when cleaning a girl's genitals is that you should clean a baby girl's vulva by wiping front to back. The idea is to wipe excrement away from the vulva, which will help prevent urinary tract infections.

Little boy's penises can simply be wiped clean. Do not try to pull the foreskin back and uncircumcised baby boys. Great care should also be taken when wiping a freshly circumcised penis.

Diaper Rash

Most babies will develop some irritation or rash during their first months due to wet diapers. The best way to treat diaper rash is to change your baby's diaper as soon as it gets wet, coupled with liberal use of diaper cream. Clean them carefully with baby wipes, making sure not to rub or scrub which will make the irritation worse. Exposing the area to air for a few minutes will help, and then apply diaper cream on and around the rash before putting it on the diaper. If the rash doesn't clear up, ask your doctor about it.

Handling The Smell

It is hilarious to watch guys gag at the sight of baby poop. Unfortunately, it's a common reaction and not funny at all when it happens to you.

BE PREPARED: keep a small bottle of Vick's Vapor Rub in the diaper bag and put a little dab on both sides of your nose, and use disposable gloves if it helps. If you have a problem, don't let anyone video you unless you want to become internet famous.

REMEMBER: Not everyone gags at the sight or smell of their baby's poop (or spit up), so please don't assume you're going to.

Use the Time to Bond

Finally, while diapering does feel like a chore, it can be an incredibly important time for bonding and learning. While your little one is captive, you should take time to talk, play and touch. One of the best ways to spend the time is for you to talk to the baby about what they're doing, creating a monologue about the sensations and the parts that are being cleaned.

NIGHTIME -- SKELETON IN THE CUPBOARD.

Sleep comes at a premium for you and your baby. That's why you might find yourself asking this question in the middle of the night: Do I need to change my baby's dirty diaper?

During the day, that's a straightforward question. But at night, it's slightly more complicated. On one hand, your baby may have soiled her diaper while sleeping (it's more than likely to happen at least once per night). And on the other hand, you don't want to wake them unnecessarily to change them. So if your baby is still asleep, should you risk waking them to change the diaper?

Luckily, the answer is simple and will mean you can get the most rest possible. Unless your baby is extremely wet or has pooped, you can probably let them sleep. Believe it or not, there's no need to wake your baby every time they wet their diaper a little. Many of today's diapers are so absorbent that your baby may be able to sleep through the night, or as long as they're capable, even if they've wetted one. When they wake up on their own, or you need to wake them for a feeding, you'll have a chance to clean them up and put on a fresh diaper. Until then, you can probably rest easy (emphasis on rest. New parents need as much as they can get!).

Now I know what you're thinking, "Okay smarty pants, I get that I don't need to change my baby's diaper every single time they wet it in the middle of the night, but what about when I do need to change them at night? What then? And can you tell me in an easily digestible listicle format?" Well, that's an oddly specific request, but don't worry, we've got you covered.

How To Get In And Out Without Disrupting Sleep

Every time you interact with your baby, you naturally want to maximize bonding time. And changing diapers, believe it or not, presents a wonderful bonding opportunity.

Turning your head away in disgust to get it over with as quickly as possible isn't what we mean. We know that you probably use this time to get some eye contact going and to communicate with your baby. You might sing a song, give a tummy raspberry, or just work your magic to make the experience fun.

But that's actually exactly how not to change a diaper in the middle of the night. Here are five things to do:

Establish a Routine

Routines are great when it comes to babies. Babies like routines because it comforts them. And parents like them because routines help set the foundation that there are certain rules to follow. Newer baby monitors like Nanit even track your baby's sleep and let you know when your bedtime routine is becoming inconsistent, as this can result in more sleepless nights for you and your child.

You may think that because your diaper change routine during the day involves eye contact and general playfulness, you should maintain the same routine at night. You can do that, but expect your baby to fully wake up if you do. Setting up a special night-time diaper change routine will help your baby go back to sleep.

Change diaper at bedtime

Changing your baby's diaper at bedtime will give you both the best chance at a full night's sleep, so consider making that a part of the nightly routine. If your baby has sensitive skin and you're worried they might develop diaper rash from a wet diaper, you can try applying diaper cream before bed. That might help keep them comfortable and asleep, and spare you both a diaper change.

Use dedicated nighttime diapers

You may also want to use the most absorbent diapers at night. During the day, these more expensive varieties might not be worth the extra price. But at night, the extra absorption could mean the difference between deep sleep and a sleepless night.

Make sure baby's diaper fits well

The fit of a diaper is paramount. That's never more important than during the night. Finding a snug diaper could be a matter of trying a handful of sizes and styles until you find one that fits your baby's body and is comfortable but won't leak. Some parents have success with cloth diapers, which can be very absorbent and comfortable.

Be in Stealth Mode

When your baby wakes during the night, the idea is to get them back to sleep as soon as possible. Just as lights and stimulation make it tough for you to fall back asleep, they do the same for your baby. Your goal is to get in and out of the room as quickly and quietly as possible, like a sneaky cat burglar.

Change Poopy Diapers

Remember, if you see (or smell) that your baby pooped their diaper, you need to change it. Whatever you do, don't turn on the overhead light. You want to keep the room dark. Installing dimmers on the lights or using a nightlight are both good options for nighttime diaper changes. Change the diaper as matter-of-factly and gently as possible, and do not look into your baby's eyes. This will only excite them. Your goal is to send the message that this is not playtime. Once you've changed the diaper, put your baby back to bed.

Expert tip: Use a wipe warmer at night. Cold wipes are more likely to wake your baby than warm ones.

Leave Wet Diapers Alone

Again, you can leave a wet diaper alone during the night, waiting until morning to change it — unless your baby's diaper is soaked through to their pajamas. If you're concerned about diaper rash, the Mayo Clinic recommends using some type of barrier ointment, one that contains petroleum jelly or zinc oxide. You can use this diaper ointment each time you change your baby's diaper, or you can use it before bed only. You also might wish to use a high-quality or overnight diaper, which should keep your baby dry and comfortable during the night.

Change Before You Feed

If your newborn baby is awake for a feeding, there are two good times to change their diaper and one not-so-good time. Change your baby before the mom change sides (or halfway through the bottle). This usually wakes babies up enough to get them to take a full feeding. If that wakes your baby too much, change their diaper first, and then feed them. If you change the diaper after you feed your baby, you risk completely waking them again.

III

STILL A DAD - SET SOME RULES AND PLAY MORE ROLES

Recently, I moderated a black men's seminar at Zahra's bookstore in Inglewood, California. The group present consisted of about 20 men and 7 women. Silly as it may sound, we figured that there's no bottom line, no official guide, no absolute authority on raising kids, so there are literally hundreds of books on how to be a good parent and raise kids right. One book says if your baby cries, pick them up. Another book says let 'em cry it out. A third book says pick them up once, then let them cry it out. A fourth... well, you get the idea. So how do you know which one is right? you must do the research and decide for yourself. However, believe it or not, your research includes following the guidelines given in this part of the book.

Also, this part is not just about your baby. It is also about you; from maintaining your sanity to balancing yor finances.

THE NEW DAD MINDSET

"Fathering is not something perfect men do, but something that perfects the man."

— FRANK PITTMAN

A few years ago, while my wife's baby bump got bigger and my daddy reading list grew longer, I felt cautiously optimistic that this parenthood thing would, somehow, suddenly click one day. The baby would come, instincts would kick in, and the transition from an established couple to a new family would be tiring but not baffling because I was preparing for fatherhood. I thought I knew what to expect the first year.

Bruh was I wrong.

This is not an attempt at what so many fathers seem to revel in: scaring the heck out of fathers-to-be with an eye-rolling mix of martyrdom and schadenfreude. This preparing for fatherhood thing isn't going to rob you of all freedoms, friendships, and fun.

But there are certainly a few things that, in retrospect, I wish I had a heads up about beforehand. Below are six of them:

Above all else: TAKE PATERNITY LEAVE.

First and foremost: if at all possible, take more than just a few days off when your baby arrives. I still have regrets about going back to work too soon after my son's birth. I implore you not to make the same mistake I did. Take as much time as feasible.

If your employer has a paternity leave policy, take the time. If your employer doesn't have a paternity leave policy, make the time. Push the envelope—it's worth it.

You're only a new dad once. Your family needs you more than your boss does right now. Just as importantly, you need them. Invest time in bonding with the baby and establishing a co-parenting dynamic that lays the groundwork for child-rearing equality.

Emails can wait. Embracing your new role as a dad cannot. Take the time, even if it means burning vacation and/or sick days. Put your visions of parenting grandeur on the shelf. Specifically, right next to the diapers, powders, ointments, and breast pump.

When my wife was six months pregnant, I couldn't wait to play catch with my son in the yard. Six months later, I couldn't wait for him to stop crying so I could get some sleep.

My point: this is a marathon, not a sprint. The whimsical Hollywood moments of fatherhood—ball games, bike rides, BBQs—are years away, and real-life doesn't have montages. But don't let your yearning for more seemingly fulfilling- parenting —the teaching moments that guide them through adolescence and into adulthood—divert you from the mission at hand. Newborn nurturing may be less glorious but it is equally necessary, and rewarding in its own right.

Stay in the now while happily anticipating more interactive parenting periods. It turns out my son needed to crawl before he could walk, and walk before he could play catch.

Listen, learn, and leave ego out of it.

All joys of new fatherhood aside, this is the greatest opportunity you've ever had to develop a valuable new skill: childcare. And you get to do it in the service of people you love. Welcome to Baby U. Your instructors include your beloved wife, parents, and in-laws.

The vast majority of early parenting is logistics. Mastering how to arrange a diaper for maximum dryness (fold the front top an inch in before fastening) is far more important than developing bigger-picture parenting perspectives.

Little humans need little things—learn them with humility.

Your reward—other than the satisfaction of dad duties well done—will be comforting, coagulating insight into how this whole baby thing works. You won't be intimidated when someone's watching you swaddle your baby. You won't be befuddled by how a car seat straps in or a stroller unfolds. It's not magic—it just takes willingness and practice

Your wife is more importto run the race effectively than you right now.

This isn't some hackneyed "happy wife, happy life" nonsense. Your marriage of equal halves has one partner who, for biological reasons, needs her spouse to be particularly helpful and supportive right now. And by "right now," I mean the first six months of parenthood, at least.

Your wife is sore, probably feeling less-than-attractive, and potentially experiencing some level of postpartum doldrums. And since you can't breastfeed, she's taking the lion's share of the overnight shift. So add exhausted to the list, too.

Your job, then, is basically "everything else."

Coddle. Clean. Cook (or in my case order takeout). Run errands, walk the dog, and stand guard against unwanted visitors. All woke-ness aside, early parenting roles revert to tradition out of necessity; she has to care for the baby right now, and you have to care for her. Do your duty—and the dishes—with honor and gratitude.

That said, don't bend so far that you end up with resentments.

Let's have a frank discussion about self-respect and marital equilibrium, because both may be tested in early parenthood—for both partners. Though new moms deserve loads of leeway, there are limits to how much they should be marginalized. Her needs—and especially the baby's—are paramount right now. But not to the point where you forfeit all respect and relevance.

Flip on the TV and you'll see how disrespected dads are these days. From Modern Family to Family Guy, the "doofus dad" stereotype permeates society. Don't let it infect your household.

You may be third fiddle right now but remember: you're still in the band. And so long as you're trying, you deserve respect; not because you're a man, mind you, but because you're a well-intending soul navigating new parenthood, too.

This is only temporary.

And by "this" I mean "all of this."

Newborns go through phases and stages with head-spinning speed. As soon as you recognize one pattern, it often gets replaced or redirected by another. Sleeping habits, feeding tendencies, what does and doesn't soothe the baby when they cry all evolve remarkably rapidly.

So if you find yourself in a particularly rough phase, relax. It will pass. And if you find yourself recognizing stages only in their twilight—before their inevitable dissipation—don't kick yourself. That happens to everyone—moms and dads alike, and especially with firstborns.

And even if, like me, you're not prone to sentimentality, do stop to soak this in. You'll only be a new dad once: the pride, the pain, the simple joys, and sleeplessness are all part of it, and all beautiful in their nascent reality.

This is all normal, and an unprecedented opportunity for growth. You are fortunate, durable, and altogether fine.

13

DEFEAT THE FUBB IN YOU

"To love oneself is the beginning of a lifelong romance."

— OSCAR WILDE

"I had about all I could stand," a colleague told his friend. "I had a new boss at work that was driving me totally nuts micromanaging everything I did and violating long-established policies in the process. My brain seemed to be bulging from the stress of the day and all I wanted that evening walking in the door was a little rest. I couldn't wait to get home, play with the kids and just unwind.

"But as I walked in the door, it was clear that a tornado had hit in our living room. Not literally, but it seemed like it. Toys were scattered everywhere, and my sweetheart was suffering from a horrible cold and headache. The three kids were tired and hungry, and there was nothing in the house to eat. And I thought that I had been the victim of a bad day so far - it only went downhill from there."

So many fathers find themselves in situations like this where the stress builds and builds until there is a breakdown. Stress meltdowns can take many forms - headaches, explosions of anger, depression and discouragement, sleeplessness, or just living with emotional pain.

Part of the solution to better handling stress is to learn some stress management techniques which would be a godsend for any father. Unfortunately, eliminating stress in our lives is not possible. But it is possible to manage the stresses that we do experience and to mitigate them so that the impact on our lives is minimized.

These ideas will help you reduce the level of stress at home and make home a place where you do want to be anytime.

Set Aside Some Family Downtime.

The pressures of modern life take their toll on a family. While work and chores are important, so are recreation and play. Make time every day for a little "daddy time" with the children. Telling bedtime stories can be a great way to relax and relieve some stress. Family rituals like family prayer, cuddle time in bed with the family, and Saturday morning breakfasts can be important times for both building relationships and reducing stress.

Make Time To Talk.

So often, stress at home is the result of failed communications. So make sure you talk with your partner and your family regularly. Plan a weekly family night so you can deal with problems before they happen. A family therapist said that his best advice for strong marriages was to set aside 30 minutes each night after the kids are in bed for mom and dad to talk together – no television, no smartphones, and no computer – just talk.

Remember good nutrition and regular exercise. Experts on stress management suggest we always make time for healthy eating and physical activity. Proper nutrition will give you good fuel to burn and exercise makes your body more efficient. Eating junk food and sitting in front of the computer all day will tend to make you tired and irritable, and increase your personal and family stress levels.

Make Time For Yourself.

In addition to giving time to your partner and family, make sure that dad's needs are met too. Participate in a favorite hobby that makes you a better man, husband, and father. Getting high or just aimlessly surfing the Internet is not as good as a little golf, hiking, reading, or working in the yard. Find what you like to do – what relaxes you - and then do more of it. And if you can involve the kids or your partner in your favorite downtime activities, all the better.

Work It Out.

Good hard physical labor can help relieve stress. Those endorphins that the body releases when you are physically active are natural mood enhancers. So get out and work in the yard if you have one. Build a project. Mow the lawn or rake the leaves. Or go help a neighbor with a project. Train for a 10K run. Hit the gym and lift a few weights or run on the treadmill. Get active and sweat a bit and you will handle the stress better.

Sharpen The Saw.

Leadership and productivity guru Stephen Covey tells about a man who was cutting wood with a dull saw. We all can recognize that such an activity is not very productive. When a friend asks him why he doesn't stop to sharpen the saw, the woodcutter says, "I am too busy sawing to stop to sharpen the saw." We all experience times like this, but our continuing to work with dull tools – mentally, emotionally, and spiritually – is pretty unproductive. So Covey recommends that we take time daily to sharpen our personal saws in four areas: mental, spiritual, emotional/social, and physical. He promises that spending one hour in these pursuits will be a powerful investment in the other 23 hours of the day.

Learn to say no.

Many of the stress factors in our family come from over-programming our time and lives. A good way to moderate the stresses that come from too much to do is to say no to the unimportant. To do that effectively, you have to define what is important and commit to that, and then say no to everything else. World-renowned Pastor Joel Osteen, who has a church in Texas to which 40,000 parishioners come weekly, has found that he has to say no to weddings and funerals, and any other events on Wednesdays and Sundays. Obviously, Sunday is the day he preaches. Wednesday is his day with God and his family first. He is a great example of practicing what he preaches and putting first things first.

Laugh.

There is no better antidote to stress and anxiety than a little laughter. One family that has learned this lesson has In their home DVDs of many years of The Cosby Show, which is a family favorite. When things get a bit stressful, this family often spends 30 minutes watching Cosby, and life is in greater perspective after they have laughed a bit. Read a little funny article or a book, tell stupid jokes, go to a comedy club with your partner, and take the time to laugh. In so many ways, laughter is the best medicine for stress.

If you need help, get it.

When stress gets overwhelming and over time affects your daily life in negative ways, get to a family counselor and get help. Fathers who don't learn to manage stress well often take it out on the people closest to them, and you just can't afford to find yourself there. Regular outbursts, abusive behavior, or loss of control are signs that you may need emotional help. Check with your employer to see if they offer an employee assistance program (EAP) or with your church to see if they have counseling programs. Consider a father's support group in your area. Find resources to be of help when you can't seem to handle them on your own.

Families are too precious to lose, and not handling stress often leads to fractured relationships, emotional and physical separation, and divorce. Keep your stress at a manageable level and make life at home more pleasant, and you will build important family relationships that last a lifetime.

14

MANAGING FINANCES

"We cannot direct the wind, but we can adjust the sails."

— DOLLY PARTON

Each year when Father's Day rolls around, I'm reminded that I wouldn't trade the experience of raising my three kids for the world. But when I think back to how naïve my wife and I once were about the costs of raising children, I can't help wishing we'd been better prepared.

As a new dad (or dad-to-be), you'd better sit down. According to the U.S. Department of Agriculture's annual Expenditures on Children by Families report, a typical middle-income family can expect to spend over $241,000 to raise a newborn child until age 18 -- and that doesn't even include prenatal care or college costs.

That said, I discovered there are two ways to run the race effectively. One way is to plan your finances, and the second way is to minimize the cost of living. I'd call the first approach "the average American masterplan" and the latter "the genius new dad approach."

Let's see how...

Average American Masterplan

Right now, you're probably more worried about getting enough sleep than funding your retirement. But at some point, you'll need to plot out a financial roadmap to ensure your family's future financial security. As one dad to another, here are a few strategies I've learned that can help

Start saving ASAP

It's hard to save for the future when you present expenses are so daunting, but it's important to start making regular contributions to several savings vehicles, even if only a few dollars at a time.

Establish an emergency fund with enough cash to cover at least six months of living expenses. If that goal seems unattainable, start small: Have $25 or $50 a month from your paycheck or checking account automatically deposited into separate savings account so you never see it, to begin with.

Even if retirement is decades away, the sooner you start saving and compounding your interest, the faster your savings will grow. If your employer offers 401(k) matching contributions, contribute at least enough to take full advantage of the match: A 50 percent match is the same as earning 50 percent interest on savings.

Once those two accounts are well established, open a 529 Qualified State Tuition Plan to start saving for your children's education.

If funding these accounts seems impossible, look for a few luxuries you could cut from your budget for six months -- lattes, going out to lunch, premium cable, etc. After six months have passed, evaluate whether they were actual "needs" or simply "wants" you can live without.

Get insured.

If your family depends on your income, you must be prepared for life's unexpected events, whether an accident, illness, unemployment, or death. Make sure you've got adequate coverage for:

Health insurance. Everyone needs medical insurance, no matter how young or healthy. Just remember: Lower-premium medical plans aren't necessarily cheaper overall; factor in copayment, deductible and prescription costs, in- and out-of-network charges, and exclusions when choosing a policy.

Homeowner/renter's insurance. Don't let theft, fire, faulty plumbing, or other catastrophes leave your family without a home or possessions. To reduce premiums, consider choosing a higher deductible. And opt for "replacement cost" vs. "actual cash value" coverage so your items will be replaced in today's dollars, rather than after depreciation has been factored in -- it's more expensive coverage but worth the extra cost.

Life insurance.

Depending on your family's size and ages, you'll probably want coverage worth at least five to 10 times your annual pay -- more, if you want to cover college costs. And don't forget to insure your spouse's life so you'll be protected as well.

Disability insurance.

Millions of Americans suffer disabilities serious enough to make them miss work for months or years at a time; yet many forego disability insurance, potentially leaving them without an income after a serious accident or illness. Learn details of your employer's sick leave and short-term disability benefits and if a long-term disability is offered, consider buying it.

Car insurance.

Almost every state requires insurance if you own or drive a car -- and for good reason: It protects you financially should you cause an accident or be hit by an uninsured driver. Make sure you have sufficient liability coverage to protect your net worth and income -- it only takes one serious accident to wipe out your savings.

Get Organized

Make sure your affairs are in order in case something should happen to you. Organize files for:

- Medical, homeowner/renter, auto, life, disability, and long-term care insurance policies.
- Banking, credit card, and loan accounts, including passwords for online account management.
- A will (and possibly a trust) outlining how you want your estate managed after death.

A durable power of attorney and health care proxy specifying who will make your financial and medical decisions if you become incapacitated. Also, a living will tells doctors which medical treatments and life-support procedures you do or don't want to be performed. If the primary assignee is your spouse, choose alternates as well, in case you're both impacted.

Birth certificate, marriage license, Social Security card, funeral and burial plans, safe deposit box information, and other important paperwork.

With all these documents, keep in mind:

Review them regularly and make updates when situations change. Make sure that designated beneficiaries for your will, life insurance, and retirement plan accurately reflect your current wishes. For example, if a beneficiary dies or a new child is born, you may want to amend the documents.

Make sure your homeowner's insurance accurately reflects inflationary increases to the value of your home and its contents.

Make backup copies of everything (and photos/videos of possessions) and store them in a few safe locations.

And finally, spend responsibly. If you buy things you don't really need or can't afford, you'll just end up having to work longer hours to pay for them -- time you could have spent watching your kids growing up.

The Genius New Dad

If you had gone through what I went through, you wouldn't mind this approach. You'll have no shame asking for help or better put... helping yourself.

When my wife and I had our first child, no one really told us about financially planning for a baby or about money-saving tips that would be helpful to a new family. We just had to wing it.

I don't want you to wing it. I want you to be prepared as possible for life with a newborn. If you already have a little one... or little ones... at home, I want this to be the motivation you need to get your finances in check

How can you afford a baby?

This is one of those "learn from my mistakes," money-saving tips for new dads. Before we had our first child, I did what any dad is supposed to do: I sold off my man toys – sports car, my collection of random sports memorabilia. But I didn't realize there was more that could be done.

The truth was that before we brought our newborn home, we should have set a budget – the same budget we would have to stick to as new parents – so that we wouldn't have to sort it out in the middle of learning to be parents.

So, make sure you do what we didn't do. Spend a few months living with the new budget before you have to. Trust me, it will save you LOTS of headaches and heartbreaks.

Nurse instead of formula

If it's physically and emotionally possible for your partner to nurse, I highly recommend it. The baby books and blogs might say that it doesn't matter, but from a financial perspective, you will thank me later.

It's estimated that families spend $1700 on formula during the first year of their child's life.

A child costs approximately $250,000. Think about the other important places you could spend that money!

Make your own baby food

Have you ever read the label on a jar of baby food? If you have, you know that this is actually much easier than it sounds. The baby food companies make money because they make it convenient for parents.

- The reality is that you can do it yourself. What are the benefits of making your own baby food?
- You will know exactly what's in the food that you're putting in your child's body.
- You will spend 1/3 the amount of money that you would spend on pre-packaged baby food.

- You will learn the names of all of those vegetables you hated as a kid.
- Get hand-me-down clothes and toys.

I'll be honest. Before I had a child, I swore up and down that I would never let him play with toys that belonged to another kid or wear clothes that had already been worn.

But I was quickly hit in the face with the sheer cost of baby toys and clothes. Along with that, I realized that a newborn grows so fast, it's nearly impossible to keep up with. Because of the savings, I took all the hand-me-downs, from friends and siblings that I could get my hands on.

Buy Used

As I said, I was hesitant to buy used clothes or let my child play with toys that weren't new. If you're similar to me in that regard, I suggest you do the math. Your kids won't care that they are playing with someone else's John Deere tractor and your pocketbook will thank you, too. Here are some great places to utilize for quality used toys and clothes:

- Facebook Marketplace
- Craigslist
- Once Upon a Child
- Local consignment shop
- Kidizen Kid Resale Marketplace
- Go To The Library

Walt Disney once said, "There is more treasure in books than in all the pirate's loot on Treasure Island."

A parent's job is to open his child's mind to the world's treasures that can only be found in books. One glance at Barnes and Noble and you'll see that buying just a few children's books can cost you over $50. When you compare $50 with the library that is… well… free… the choice gets pretty clear. The question is why would you spend all that money on something that you could just get for free?

Eat At Home

In the last two decades, people have become more ambivalent about cooking and eating at home. In fact, one study discovered a family that had unknowingly accrued $30,000 in credit card debt JUST from eating out.

Along with a decrease in cooking at home, people are increasingly eating out for lunch every day. And if a person were to eat out every day for a year, spending $10 each time, they would spend a minimum of $2,500.

Don't fall into the same trap as a large portion of Americans. Just like you could spend 1/3 less on baby food if you make your own, you would spend 1/3 less on food if you eat at home. And, on the plus side, your savings will outweigh the annoyance of having to do dishes!

Buy In Bulk

Finally, if you have the resources and access to Costco, you can cut the cost of having children by saving at least 20% on your purchases. How? Buying in bulk. In addition to financial savings, there are other benefits:

- Less packaging means you don't have to manage as much waste.
- Collecting a lot of the essentials means you are prepared for an emergency. There's no need for extra stress in the face of an emergency when there's a newborn at home.
- Buying in bulk means fewer trips to the store. Enough said.

Children are expensive blessings. They bring joy to our lives while, at the same time, costing us around $250,000. If you do the math, it's easy to get overwhelmed and think, "How will I afford a baby?"

I've been there before and I know that just thinking about bringing home a newborn can bring stress into your life. But, trust me. If you can put some of these money-saving tips for new dads into practice, you can take hold of what might feel like something out of your control.

15

COACHING YOUR CHILD

"It is easier to build strong children than to repair broken men"

— FREDERICK DOUGLAS

Have you ever wondered how independent your child actually is or would be? Will your child be able to look after themselves if left alone for a while? Do you think your child is well-equipped with essential life skills to face the world?

Remember those times you would ask about spending the night at a friends' house or about going over to someone's house to play? How many times did your parents say, "No. They are a bad influence on you?" If they never said it, they were thinking it!

Think about it!

It's absolutely important for children to learn more than just academically. And no, enrolling them in various activity classes isn't enough either. Your children would be happier to learn some of these skills from you.

Before we get started, please be reminded that there are no one-fits-all skills to teach children as this will vary due to various factors, such as gender, age, location, etc. You should carefully read and decide the best skills you think your child needs to know.

So, let's look at a few skills that are essential for any growing child to learn in order for them to find it easy to deal with adulthood and how you can teach your child these skills.

BASIC SELF-DEFENCE:

I'm sure you'll agree that in today's world especially, safety is of utmost importance, and developing self-defence not only makes the child feel more independent, but also more confident.

Basic self-defence is a must — be it for your son or your daughter. Most schools these days invest in teaching basic self-defence to children. But if your child's school does not, don't hesitate to send them for classes outside.

FIRST-AID AND THE IMPORTANCE OF HEALTH:

You can't expect to always be around whenever your child gets hurt, a bite or a rash! So how about empowering them such that they are able to take care in case of an emergency until they reach a grown-up?

This is essentially something the child's schooling should cover but I strongly encourage its reinforcement at home by teaching your child essential first aid steps.

And this you can do by showing them a first aid kit and its contents. Children are, after all, excellent learners!

Another important skill is teaching your child to take care of their health. Instead of forcing your child to eat vegetables, talk to them about health risks in eating junk food all the time and explain how the healthy food will benefit them in a way that they can apply to themselves.

For example, for a kid interested in sports, talk about foods that give them increased stamina and agility, enabling them to play better at their sport.

For kids that care about physical appearance traits like hair, talk about the importance of Omega-3 fatty acids and the foods that contain it.

MAKE THEM DO THEIR OWN WORK:

Let's face it. When our kids grow up, they are very likely to leave home to pursue their education or career. And if they aren't taught responsibility and daily-living skills today, it would be a problem for them in the future.

Most parents run around doing everything for their children so much so that the child doesn't get involved in anything. This shouldn't be the case.

Be it putting their school bag together or taking the plate to the kitchen, ensure your child is 'responsible' for their work. Teach these skills now, before it's too late! And there will be another helping hand at home, isn't it?

PRO TIP: You can also try an activity box like Flintobox to make a child learn and develop skills independently. The activities in Flintobox are highly educational where children learn concepts and life skills through play!

HOW TO MANAGE TIME:

You're probably wondering how. Well, you can do this by getting your kid to claim responsibility for their own time.

Do this by getting them an alarm clock that they can use to wake up on time for school, instead of you waking them up.

Get them a planner to use to track their school work and other extra-curricular work and to keep track of what needs to be done by when.

When they do this, they will automatically begin to allow specific amounts of time for play and for work.

DECISION-MAKING SKILLS:

Education, career, life partners — there are so many important decisions we need to make in our lives. How about instilling the skill of making appropriate decisions at an early age itself in your child?

Here's how to — teach them in small and simple ways how to make wise decisions. Start by asking them to choose between 2 activities or games; 2 different types of clothes; 2 different food items, etc.

Once this happens, the child will understand the consequences that each decision causes. So guide your child through the process, help them weigh the advantages and disadvantages before they make their decision!

MANAGING MONEY & BASIC BUDGETING:

This is quite a basic one among life skills. Give your children a certain amount of pocket money every week or every two weeks that they have to use for their expenses.

If they wish to buy something a little more expensive, ask them to save up their pocket money to buy it.

Or, you can lend them a helping hand by telling them that for every chunk of money they save, you'll add a certain amount of money to their fund for buying the product.

This will motivate them more. I think the concept of comparative shopping also comes under the concept of teaching your child about budgeting.

Tell them why you choose comparatively cheaper options sometimes. When they want to buy a few things when you go shopping, encourage them to pick one or two items if they're of the same kind.

This kind of budgeting training develops a habit in your child to not waste money and to respect its value.

I believe understanding the importance of money and managing it is something that every child above the age of 10 should know.

They are introduced to the concept of money from the age of 7 in school via subjects like Maths but nobody teaches them the importance and relevance of budgeting, planning, saving and the real value of money as they have never handled money in real life.

Open a bank account for your child, ask them to deposit some money every month (money received as gifts or if they help out in the house with some tasks you could pay them a small amount.) This will inculcate the habit of saving and appreciating money.

SHOPPING SKILLS:

Always take your child grocery shopping with you. Once your child knows where the different categories of items are shelved, give them a basket and ask them to get a few easy-to-find things for you.

You can also keep your kid in charge of buying a few things every month. Examples of this would be snacks and juices. Once done, teach them how to pay for it!

And the most important point — don't forget to model smart shopping yourself!

INVOLVE THEM IN SIMPLE COOKING:

Children can cook, too! Don't you agree?

And you can start with simple things! Teach your child how to make their own peanut butter and jam sandwiches, teach them how to butter a slice of bread, and how to make a salad.

Have them tear up greens, squeeze lemons, and put chopped vegetables together to make a salad.

You can also get them to help you with baking, with handing you ingredients while you cook or with keeping the kitchen table clean while you're preparing a meal.

IMPORTANCE OF ENVIRONMENTAL PRESERVATION:

Instilling the importance of environment and sustainability at an early age will teach your child to be more loving towards the planet. Teach your kid why preserving the environment is essential by making small lifestyle changes at home. Get them to practise eco-friendly habits in everything they do.

You can also make them do environmental activities such as gardening and collecting waste to throw in a bin. If you have a yard, give them a portion of the yard to plant whatever they like in.

Help them sow seeds and make it their responsibility to water the plants. If you don't have a yard, you can always use planting pots.

FINISH TASKS INDEPENDENTLY:

Let your children do their own tasks. Let them pack their own school bag, make their own bed, and even pack their own lunch!

You can do this by making each task a bit exciting by helping them out. Buy them new bedding and cushions themed around a cartoon or movie they love.

Have a sandwich station or a pancake station for breakfast with cut-up fruits, jams, syrup, spreads, etc, so they can make their own plate and eat it the way they like.

HOW TO INTERACT WITH PEOPLE:

We've all taught children about stranger danger but this doesn't make much logical sense considering every person we're close to as adults was a stranger to us at some point.

Instead, teach your children to do exactly what adults do. Teach them to differentiate between good strangers and bad strangers. Teach them how to interact with good strangers.

Teach them how to make friends, how to be friendly to good adults, and just how they should go about interacting with these people.

If you think about it, a task that we do every single day is to be engaged in interaction with people. If we don't teach children this at a young age, they may not develop positive social skills.

CLEANING AND OTHER HOUSEHOLD CHORES:

Now I know what you're thinking. Getting kids to get involved in cleaning activities is really hard! We agree. But we assure you that your effort will be well worth it!

Start small by just asking them to keep their room clean, make their bed, and make sure everything they own is in its right place. You can then ask them to clean the dishes that they use to eat after eating as well.

You can ask them to dust the tables one day and ask them to take the trash out on another; you can also ask them to set the table in whichever way they think looks the best and ask them to get creative with it.

Ask them to participate in chores such as these to help you out or in exchange for their allowance.

It's important to practise these activities both in the context of an allowance and out of it, so your child learns to just help out without being given anything in return, too.

BASIC ETIQUETTES & HOW TO ORDER AT RESTAURANTS:

Teach your kid about how to behave at a restaurant and how to place an order. Ask them to place their own orders and decide on what they want to eat on their own.

Also, teach them how to eat with a knife and fork, how to place the knife and fork on the plate once they're done eating, and on how to tip the waiters.

HOW TO USE MAPS:

Going somewhere? Start off by teaching your kids the routes around your house and test this by asking them to direct you home or to school the next time you're dropping them.

You can then ensure that your child learns how to read a map, and also teach them how to use a GPS and follow its instructions.

BASICS OF TRAVELLING:

Aside from navigation, your child should know travelling basics.

From learning to ride a cycle to learning how to use public transport, make sure your child knows how to do these things along with routes.

Teach them how to buy metro or bus tickets, teach them the basics of which metro train or bus goes to your house from school. These are important skills that your child will need for later as well as for emergencies.

LOOKING AT SITUATIONS FROM OTHERS' PERSPECTIVES:

When your child comes to you about a problem that he or she had with their friend or a problem that they witnessed, encourage them to look at the situation that took place from the perspective of others.

Even explain the emotional reactions of people every chance you get. Explain why someone is sad or angry.

This increases their problem-solving abilities and their level of understanding of the people around them greatly.

RESILIENCE & ADAPTABILITY:

Another important skill would be to teach your child to be resilient. How you can do this is by ensuring you don't feed your child with solutions all the time.

Empower your child to problem-solve by themselves so that they're ready to face challenges as and when they come. They must learn resilience to adapt to different changes and different environments.

Make sure you have an open channel of communication to understand what your child is going through and help them out – and of course, as a parent, you too must model resilient behaviour at home!

CONCLUSION

There are experiences we go through in life, that change us forever. Fatherhood, for me, was one of them. It changed my perspectives on many things, including the role that women play in the furtherance of life.

Therefore, if you got nothing else out of this book than the fact that you need to play a larger role in your partner's pregnancy, then I will call this book a success. Be there, be present. Go to the appointments and the classes and take an active part in what is going on. Times have changed. No longer is it acceptable for fathers to just sit back and allow their wives to take care of the children. Show her that you understand that.

I know that we've talked a lot about how you can help her, but it's important to remember that this is your baby too. Do not for one second think that you have it as hard as she does at any point in the process of raising a baby, but do remember that you are important and you still play a vital role in your baby's upbringing. Too often, I see men taking the backseat to their partners when it comes to babies. And yes, while she does have a very strong opinion about how she wants things to do be done, that doesn't mean that you can't give your two cents too. If you want something that your lady doesn't or vice versa, speak up. The baby is just as much yours as it is hers.

Be a part of the process, not just a spectator. Be there. She will appreciate it, eventually. She will love and appreciate you all the more for making the effort. Though, the fact that you're using this book and searching for ways to help on the internet is already a good sign.

And, lastly, remember that you're important too. Take care of yourself, seek help, take breaks, and remember that fatherhood is not something perfect men do. Rather, it is something that perfects the man. If all you did today was to wake up and try again, I'm proud of you!

QUICK NOTE

Positive reviews from awesome customers like you help others to feel confident about choosing this book too. Could you take 60 seconds to go to and share your happy experiences?

Should you have any concerns or reccomendations about this book, our email is always open. You can reach out to **book-contact@alfie-thomas.com.** We will be forever grateful.

Thank you in advance for helping us out!

ABOUT THE AUTHOR

Alfie Thomas is a father of three, lecturer, and a software engineer. He was raised by a struggling single mother in London, who had to work two jobs to make ends meet. Alfie grew up with an intense fear of becoming a parent himself, because he feared that he would have the same struggles as his own mother.

When his now wife became pregnant at age 27, Alfie experienced all-new parenting anxiety and found it difficult to sleep at night for many months following the birth of their daughter. Eventually, they welcomed two more children into their family!

It's been just over six years since they became parents and things are looking bright for the future as Alfie has learned how to be a good dad while also being successful.

REFERENCES

babycentre. (n.d.). What I wish I'd known about becoming a dad. Retrieved from babycentre.co.uk: https://www.babycentre.co.uk/a1046757/what-i-wish-id-known-about-becoming-a-dad

Brott, A. A. (2015). The Expectant Father: The Ultimate Guide to Dads-to-Be . Abbeville Press.

Greenberg, G. (2004). Be Prepared: A Practical Handbook for New Dads. Simon & Schuster.

Griffin, R. M. (2013). Advice for Expectant Fathers. Retrieved from WebMD: https://www.webmd.com/men/features/advice-for-expectant-fathers

Karen Gill, M. (2020, March 26). Preparing for Fatherhood: 16 Ways to Get Ready to Become a Dad. Retrieved from healthline.com: https://www.healthline.com/health/preparing-for-fatherhood

Kinsner, K. (2017, May 16). Becoming a Dad: Advice for Expectant Fathers. Retrieved from zerotothree: https://www.zerotothree.org/resources/1838-becoming-a-dad-advice-for-expectant-fathers

Kulp, A. (2018). We're Pregnant! The First Time Dad's Pregnancy Handbook. Rockridge Press (April 24, 2018).

M.D, L. B., & Joe Borgenicht. (n.d.). The Baby Owner's Manual: Operating Instructions, Trouble-Shooting Tips, and Advice on First-Year Maintenance (Owner's and Instruction Manual).

Masters, M. (2020, July 09). For Expecting Dads and Partners. Retrieved from whattoexpect: https://www.whattoexpect.com/pregnancy/expecting-father/

Miller, M. M. (n.d.). Basics Of Pregnancy. Retrieved from dummies.com: dummies.com

Neha Pathak, M. (2021, March 19). Dad's to-Do List: Getting Ready for Baby. Retrieved from webmd.com: https://www.webmd.com/baby/dads-to-do-list-getting-ready-for-baby

Pediatrics, A. A. (2020). Your Baby's First Year: Fifth Edition . Bantam.

Pfeiffer, J. (2011). Dude, You're Gonna Be a Dad!: How to Get (Both of You) Through the Next 9 Months. Adams Media.

whattoexpect. (2018 , August 17). 6 Surprising Pregnancy Symptoms — for Dads! Retrieved from whattoexpect: https://www.whattoexpect.com/pregnancy/photo-gallery/surprising-pregnancy-symptoms-for-dads.aspx

Wilson, H. (2018, March 23). DADS BATHING KIDS IS GOOD FOR EVERYONE. Retrieved from daddilife: https://www.daddilife.com/dads-bathing-kids-good-everyone/

It's a beautiful and exciting time for the entire family. You are about to enter into an amazing journey of fatherhood, but first, you need to prepare yourself mentally and physically. This 134-page boo, "THE FIRST FATHER: The Expectant Survival Guide For First-time Dads Through pregnancy Journey" is here to help you step by step in every aspect of your life as a dad-to-be.

It is a comprehensive guide to all the aspects of parenting for both expectant dads and first-time fathers. It covers every aspect related to pregnancy, childbirth, and early childhood roles in a simple language that can be understood by anyone.

Fun Fact:

The First Father: The Expectant Survival Guide For First-Time Dads Through Pregnancy Journey focuses on helping first-time expectant fathers to understand what they are going through and how to make the best of it. The book has been written out of my personal experience as well as experiences shared by other fathers. It is safe to say that this book will help you to make decisions on your own without any kind of confusion or doubt.

The book is divided into three parts. The first part talks about pregnancy and how you can support your pregnant partner during pregnancy. We called it the pregnancy superstar because you will become a champion by the time your little one is born. The second part discusses father-child bonding through special skills, such as diaper-changing guides, feeding, and bathing your newborn. Did we leave out other special tips, such as the new dad survival kit and cheatsheet? Of course not! You are covered in all angles of surviving fatherhood. The final part focused on how you can take care of your mental health, get your finances in order, and the general rules of child upbringing.

SOME HEADLINES IN THE BOOK:

- The story of How I Became a Father

PART 1:

- The Pregnancy Superstar
- Basic Knowledge Of Pregnancy
- Prepare Now Or Pay Later
- Getting Your **S Ready
- Helping Mommy To Save The Baby
- Your Partner's Mind Exposed!
- The P's And Q's Of Pregnancy
- Some Sex Positions You Could Try
- Things To Avoid (The Don'ts Of Pregnancy)
- The New Dad Cheatsheet

- Transition With Baby From Hospital To Home

PART 2:

- New Dad Survival Kit
- Baby Registry - Must-Have Items
- Designing A Baby Nursery In 4 Steps
- Playmate - Growing A Bond
- How To Feed Your Tot
- Bathing And Dressing A Newborn
- Becoming A Diaper-Changing Machine
- Nightime – Skeleton In The Cupboard

PART 3:

- The New Dad Mindset
- How To Defeat The Fubb In You
- Managing Your Finances
- Coaching Your Child.

You're one click away from unlocking your best father-hood potential...

Printed in Great Britain
by Amazon

81403900R00135